Words like Water

CATERINA FUGAZZOLA

Words like Water

*Queer Mobilization and Social
Change in China*

TEMPLE UNIVERSITY PRESS
Philadelphia • Rome • Tokyo

TEMPLE UNIVERSITY PRESS
Philadelphia, Pennsylvania 19122
tupress.temple.edu

Library of Congress Cataloging-in-Publication Data

Names: Fugazzola, Caterina, 1987– author.
Title: Words like water : queer mobilization and social change in China /
  Caterina Fugazzola.
Description: Philadelphia : Temple University Press, 2023. | Includes
  bibliographical references and index. | Summary: "This book uses
  ethnography, interview data, and discourse analysis from organizations
  in the People's Republic of China advocating for greater acceptance of
  queer identities to show how tactics that emphasize family, harmony, and
  sacrifice fare better in context than those that emphasize individual
  rights and flourishing"— Provided by publisher.
Identifiers: LCCN 2023003800 (print) | LCCN 2023003801 (ebook) | ISBN
  9781439921463 (cloth) | ISBN 9781439921470 (paperback) | ISBN
  9781439921487 (pdf)
Subjects: LCSH: Sexual minorities—China—Social conditions. | Sexual
  minorities—Political activity—China. | Gender identity—Social
  aspects—China. | Gender identity—Political aspects—China. | Sexual
  orientation—Social aspects—China. | Sexual orientation—Political
  aspects—China. | Social change—China.
Classification: LCC HQ73.3.C6 F84 2023 (print) | LCC HQ73.3.C6 (ebook) |
  DDC 306.760951—dc23/eng/20230515
LC record available at https://lccn.loc.gov/2023003800
LC ebook record available at https://lccn.loc.gov/2023003801

To all my families.

Contents

Acknowledgments

This book has been a long journey spanning three continents, as many languages, and innumerable communities who provided me with invaluable support and motivation every step of the way. I am eternally grateful for everyone who has been a part of this adventure. It would not have happened without you.

I made it here in no small part thanks to the incredible teachers and mentors I have been lucky to encounter along my path. When I was still a high school orange-mohawked punk rock misfit, Antonella Barbagallo taught me to love and respect language—at this point, I think we can confidently say you won the battle against my stubborn refusal to see the value in linguistic analysis. Cristina Re knew that Italy was boxing me in well before I did and always pushed me toward new challenges and new horizons. You are the reason I started studying Chinese in the first place, and look at where that led me. Thank you for believing in me even when I was impossible.

My love for studying Chinese took me to Venice, a city that will always have a piece of my heart. So many people made those years magical beyond words. I am so grateful to the Rio Marin crew, to the classroom friendships cemented in Campo Santa Margherita, and, of course, to the delightful presence of Le Maschere. A special token of appreciation to Gloria, who taught me to love the chaotic mess of the canals and the smell of fresh bread in the middle of the night and the taste of the cherry tomatoes from the boat. I am also forever grateful to the magic of Venice for creating the perfect set of circumstances for the beginning of one of my longest and most treasured friendships. Montagnina, you have been a distant and yet incredibly close presence throughout all my years in college, graduate school, and all the way to the present. I love you to death, and that fateful choice to "just meet up for a quick spritz and then we will go back home" on a random night in 2006 was one of the best decisions I have ever made.

Moving from Ca' Foscari University to the University of San Francisco opened up a whole new universe for me. It took me a while to figure out the strange world where university professors led graduate seminars instead of lecturing hundreds of students and where they routinely talked to me, valued my opinions, and challenged my ideas. Christopher Moreman was the first person to show me the fun and possibilities of academia, and he was my first academic publishing mentor. Thank you for teaching me there is a way to write to academics about zombies and horror movies. Doowan Lee was one of my greatest supporters in San Francisco, and he was my rock while I was applying to PhD programs. Thank you for showing me what true love for teaching looks like. And thank you for all the dinners and barbecues that helped me keep my sanity during PhD application season.

Perhaps the most significant decision I made at USF was that of sneaking into a class I was not really supposed to take and thus meeting Dorothy Kidd. Our conference in Uppsala remains one of the fondest memories of my academic life. You have been the most kind and patient mentor, and you have taught me what it means to deeply care about the communities I study. When we met, I had no idea what a PhD in the United States even entailed, and I would have never considered going down that road if it weren't for you. Thank you. I am also thankful for your class because without it I would not have met Elaine Venter, and my life would have been so much worse if I hadn't. Elaine, years after USF your encouragement and energy as we were both working our way through the challenges of doctoral work kept me going and reminded me how much fun research can be. Three cheers to doing serious work without taking ourselves too seriously.

Being at the University of Chicago has been the most challenging and rewarding experience of my life. I am lucky to have found a community of friends that have been there with me every step of the way. A cheer goes to the survivors of my disappearing cohort, Alex Brewer, Sophie Fajardo, Nathan Gonzalez, Wen Xie—we made it, and we are still going strong. Kanyi Huang, you have moved on to better things, but this research owes a great deal to you and to the serendipitous coffee conversation that started it all. Xiaogao Zhou, you have been one of the biggest supporters of this project since the day we fortuitously connected on WeChat in 2017. When I was writing my dissertation, you and Yuchen Yang probably ended up reading more chapter drafts than my committee. Thank you both for your endless patience with all my language questions. Also, you don't know this quite yet because I am writing these acknowledgments before getting the page proofs, but I will 100 percent ask you both to help me read through them and look for typos, and I am 100 percent sure you will say yes because you are kind humans and good friends. So thank you for that.

Melissa Osborne, you were my departmental half and the cat to my dog throughout our PhD years, and I love that our book-writing steps have been in such perfect sync. You'd better get a cover soon because we need to plan a double party with book cakes. We are fancy like that now. I love you, friend; you and Hannah and the whole of Osbornia still give me hope for the future. I can't wait to come feed deer again. I promise I will be extremely chill about it.

My deepest gratitude goes to my two lifelines, Hanisah Binte Abdullah Sani and Sneha Annavarapu. My dissertation and, subsequently, this book would not have come together without you. You caught me when I was in free fall, and if I made it to the finishing line, it is only because of your support. You managed to make me smile during the hardest summer of my life and gave me the strength to laugh at myself and to keep going. I feel so lucky to have you in my life. Thank you for not letting me run to the Rockies. I forgive you for moving so far away from me and promise to come visit and eat all the food Singapore has to offer.

This book is born out of my dissertation work, and I couldn't have asked for a better committee than Elisabeth Clemens, Kristen Schilt, and Dingxin Zhao. Working with you has been a dream, and I am so grateful for all your support throughout my doctoral adventure. Dingxin, you were one of the first people to help me figure out how to survive my barely funded first years in the program. Thank you for pushing me to think critically and for helping me turn my curiosity into sociological questions. Kristen, you have been so much more than a mentor throughout my years at the University of Chicago. I couldn't have done this without you. You made me a better teacher, writer, sociologist, and academic. Thank you for reminding me to breathe and for always being there for me. You believed in me when I was ready to give up, and I can never thank you enough for that. Lis, you have been the best dissertation chair I could have ever asked for. Your patience, support, and terrifyingly sharp questions helped me make this project what it is now. Thank you for always pushing me to think deeply about the significance of my findings.

So many other people contributed to making the University of Chicago feel like home throughout the years, and they cheered me on as my research slowly morphed into this book. I am indebted to my work family in the Master of Arts Program in the Social Sciences (MAPSS) in its entirety—you gave me purpose, pushed me to be better, and taught me to laugh through the stress and challenges of the job. I don't think I will ever again work with such an incredible group of people who love and respect and care for each other so much. Mark Hansen, Chad Cyrenne, Darcy Heuring, E. G. Enbar, Tekeisha Yelton-Hunter, Samantha Fan, John McCallum, Tori Gross, Ella Wilhoit, Dawn Herrera, and Amit Anshumali—thank you for everything, and for being the amazing humans that you are. Sorry I yelled at you during our Overcooked sessions. I miss you all—as you can probably tell by the fact that I constantly show up uninvited at MAPSS events. Dawn, I wish I could use emojis in these acknowledgments because your daily motivational texts in December 2021 are a big part of why I was able to actually finish revising the manuscript in time. And a particularly huge thank-you to Samantha and Frank, who adopted me during the long pandemic months, fed me delicious home-cooked meals, and helped me keep my sanity during isolation. I could not have asked for a better pod.

I am so lucky to have found a wonderful new home and community in the Global Studies Program. Kimberly Hoang, Callie Maidhof, and Lee Price, thank you for your support, your patience, and your suggestions on book titles, fonts, and cover arrangements. You are a dream team, and I look forward to many more GS adventures, events, and hilariously miscalculated tamale orders. Callie, you deserve a special thank-you for being not only a great colleague but also an amazing friend. Here is to future food explorations, board game nights, and many, many more episodes of Buffy.

Three separate centers played, and continued to play, a large role in my University of Chicago journey. The Center for the Study of Gender and Sexuality (CSGS) has been my second home here, and I want to thank all the incredible people who make that place special. Bonnie Kanter, Tate Brazas, and Gina Olson, you are the beating heart of CSGS and hands down the best event organizers on campus. I am thankful to everyone who was involved in the Gender and Sexuality Workshop and Working Group while I was a student, particularly Annie Heffernan, Omie Hsu, and Agatha Slupek. I also owe a great debt to the Writing Center and, particularly, to Linda Smith, Kathy Cochran, and Margaret Fink. I am a better writer, teacher, and mentor because of you. And I am grateful for the Media, Arts, Data, and Design (MADD) Center and for the brilliant humans who made it possible. A particular thanks goes to Patrick Jagoda and Ashlyn Sparrow. Thank you for introducing me to some of the best videogames I know. This book benefited tremendously from long gaming sessions in the midst of frenetic bursts of writing and editing.

After over ten years in the city, I can no longer ignore the fact that Chicago feels as much like my home as Milan. So many people contribute to this feeling, and I want to acknowledge a particular group that—despite being a relatively recent entry into my life—has already become a vital part of who I am here. To my Italo-Chicagoan community: I love you. Thank you for all the laughter and the cooking nights and the shameless calling me out for being a grandma. Sara Dallavalle, Leonardo Cabrini, Giacomo Melani, Alessandro Minnucci, Valentina Moro, and Daniele Biffanti—here is to many more pasta nights and many more refusals to go out dancing with you. I'll hang out with my Italo-Chicagoan nieblings, who also deserve to be acknowledged: Nina, Ercole Pierino, and Yoshi, you are welcome to stay with me anytime. Please stop opening all my closets at night; it's creepy.

This book would have probably never seen the light of day, and most definitely not as quickly as it did, had it not been for Ryan Mulligan at Temple University Press. Ryan, I am so thankful you took a chance on me by reaching out at that American Sociological Association (ASA) conference so many years ago now. I had no idea what I was doing then, barely had a dissertation outline, and the chapter I was presenting was a hot mess. And yet you believed in the project, followed up with me after I completed it, and held my hand and guided me every step of the way as that original mess turned into a coherent project. Thank you so much for everything you did. And a huge thank you to the anonymous reviewers who read my manuscript and offered kind words, fair critiques, and helpful suggestions to turn this book into what it is right now.

This research was made possible by the financial support of the Chiang Ching-Kuo Foundation, the Social Science Division, the Center for the Study of Gender and Sexuality, the Center for East Asia Studies, the Alumni Club of Italy, the University of Chicago Beijing Center, and the Pozen Family Center for Human Rights Research.

While working on this project I could always count on the unwavering support from my family, feline and human. Dina, Tolo, Spritz, Napo, and Nitro, I miss you dearly, and I know you would be proudly ignoring me if you were here. Dalia, I guess I like you even if you hate me. Fitz, you are the floofiest weirdo and please realize you are a humungous giant of a cat. Stop hiding under the comforter. It's a little embarrassing. Ziggy&Bau, your aunty loves you dearly even though you are hopeless. And a special thanks to Loki and Hela, my two goblins who came into my life during the writing mayhem and who have kept me grounded with their unstoppable mischief.

I owe much to the human counterparts to this feline assemblage. Andrea and Valeria, after years of you making fun of me for taking so long to finish my PhD I can finally say, Where are your books? And I won't accept parenthood as an excuse, though you do get points for creating one of my favorite humans on this planet. Uli, your gia loves you, but you need to slow down this whole growth process. Last time I saw you, you were already speaking in full sentences. I cannot face the reality you might be able to read by the time this book comes out.

Lastly, the deepest thanks go to my parents, to whom I owe everything I am. Thank you for your love and for always being there for me no matter how far I manage to escape. I never say this enough, but I love you more than anything.

I cannot name them here, but the people who made this research possible are all the *tongzhi*, *lala*, *tongxinglian*, and *qu'er* who welcomed this Italian lala into their community and their families. Thank you for sharing your lives with me and for trusting me to do justice to your stories.

A Note on Terminology

Throughout this study, I use *tongzhi* as an inclusive identity term that refers to nonheterosexual and gender nonconforming identities in the People's Republic of China. Like all identity terms, tongzhi is not unproblematic. As I discuss in Chapter 1, while its literal translation to "comrade" is gender neutral, the term is sometimes used to indicate a gay man and juxtaposed to *lala*, a term usually meaning lesbian. There are times in which "tongzhi community" can be approximated to "Chinese LGBT community" and other times in which tongzhi is used in contrast to LGBT. I tried to honor my participants' preferred identification labels throughout my research, which means that I sometimes refer to my informants as tongzhi—at times specifying whether the informant identified as female tongzhi or male tongzhi—but other times I rely on other terms, including *lala*, *tongxinglian* (homosexual), or *qu'er* (queer). While following the terminology employed by my respondents, I also tried to keep the use of identity labels fairly consistent throughout the work, relying on tongzhi as the default term to refer to the community as a whole.

Words like Water

Introduction

It is a warm August afternoon in the summer of 2017, and I am chatting with a few *tongzhi* friends as we walk through some rather empty streets in Chaoyang District. In a few hours, this clubbing area will be bursting with loud music and the sidewalks packed, but for now, our small group moves unhindered in front of the mostly closed restaurants and bars. We are heading toward Destination, a well-known club in Beijing, but we are not going there to dance. Tonight is the opening night of a temporary exhibit held on the second level of the club, a project months in the making. The exhibit is titled *In Search of Lost Time: Queer Memories from Beijing* (追忆似水年华: 北京的酷儿记忆), and it is a collection of materials from some of the most prominent tongzhi artists and groups active in the capital since the early 1990s. The title of the exhibit is an explicit reference to Marcel Proust, and its significance is explained on the opening wall panel that welcomes visitors near the entrance:

> We borrowed the name of a book that battles against oblivion, *In Search of Lost Time* by the late-nineteenth-century French writer Marcel Proust. The worries about the constant passing and erosion of things haunt us, while precious memories hide

away from the conscious efforts to retrieve. The absenting forces of censorship and passing time, as well as the materiality of queer lives and queer stories, remind us of the urgency to preserve and archive queer history.

Walking through the exhibit forces visitors to be confronted with the juxtaposition of presences and absences: empty frames hang next to preserved pamphlets, postcards, and memorabilia; newspaper articles from Hong Kong detail the struggles of a lesbian couple who tried to no avail to register their marriage at the Beijing registry; and memories of censored film festivals occupy empty spaces next to prizes that were instead awarded at subsequent ones. The collection is purposefully designed to tell a fragmentary, incomplete history of the tongzhi movement, exposing the inevitable gaps left by objects lost to censorship and time.

Despite the explicit themes of absences and erasures, however, the exhibit is not about loss. For almost every artifact, present or missing, a QR code connects viewers to a short audio file stored on a designated WeChat account. The files are a collection of narratives, stories, and recollections of events and pivotal turning points in the history of tongzhi organizing. Film directors recount their struggles to organize the first tongzhi film festival, actors talk about the stage props used in the first play produced for and by the tongzhi community in Beijing, and founders of some of the key organizations currently active in the People's Republic of China (PRC) narrate the beginnings of their groups. When taken as a whole, the collection of fragments tells a story of incomplete representation but also of change, visibility, and creative strategies to achieve both.

A large section of the exhibit is dedicated to "first times" and includes items such as the signature sheet from the first tongzhi "internet meeting" in 1998, in which activists teamed up to publish information on AIDS prevention on various websites. On an adjacent wall, photographs from the 1995 World Conference on Women in Beijing bring viewers back to the first time a lesbian tent was included at a United Nations nongovernmental organization (NGO) forum. Prominently displayed on one of the walls is the official business license obtained by the first organization to provide tongzhi with a physical community center, the Beijing LGBT Center (北京同志中心 *Beijing Tongzhi Zhongxin*) in 2008. Notably, the name on the license reads, "Beijing Pink Cultural Communication, Ltd." (桃红文化传播有限公司 *Taohong wenhua chuanbo youxian gongsi*) to circumvent potential issues connected to the term *tongzhi*. While showing these historical firsts, messages on the walls encourage viewers to resist a desire to romanticize the past and to look instead toward the future: "[The purpose of this exhibit section] is not to put 'the first' on a pedestal, but to look at it as a point of departure. What has changed since that first time?"

Much has changed since those first meetings in the late 1990s. China officially "decriminalized"[1] same-sex behavior in 1997, and homosexuality was deleted from the list of mental diseases in 2001. As many exhibit visitors proudly point out to me, gone are the days of clandestine meetings in parks and public bathrooms, and—thanks to the development of the internet—gone is the feeling of being alone with no community support. In the ten years between 2007 and 2017, the number of tongzhi organizations has grown from a handful of small groups to hundreds of organizations,[2] some of which count thousands of members. Social acceptance of nonnormative sexualities has grown (Pan and Huang 2013; UNDP 2016), and while representation on state media is still limited, the tongzhi community is no longer confined to the invisibility of the early 1990s (Huang 2018). As if to underline the change, a China Global Television Network (CGTN)[3] crew is filming the opening night of the exhibit for a segment dedicated to civil society, NGOs, and citizen engagement.

The growth in visibility and public acceptance of the tongzhi community has not run parallel to increased political opportunities for groups and NGOs. The opposite is in fact true—opportunities for civil society political engagement have been steadily shrinking since the mid-2010s (Fu and Distelhorst 2017; Lei 2018; S. Zhao 2016). Under the leadership of Xi Jinping, grassroots groups have been facing higher levels of policing and censorship, particularly on social media (Lei 2018). Xi's presidency has proven particularly sensitive on matters related to rights, by presenting rights-based discourses as an ideological attack perpetuated by Western forces in an effort to undermine the Chinese Communist Party (CCP) (Lei 2018, 172; S. Zhao 2016). From a political standpoint, tongzhi groups are somewhat sheltered from scrutiny as they occupy a liminal gray area delineated by the official state policy of "not encouraging, not discouraging, and not promoting" homosexual behavior, an approach that captures the overarching disinterest of the Chinese state in tongzhi-related matters. This political invisibility is a double-edged sword for tongzhi organizers—while it grants them a certain degree of freedom, it also makes it difficult for them to know where the boundaries between acceptable and unacceptable behavior lie.

Given the liminal, somewhat paradoxical political position of tongzhi groups in China, it is perhaps unsurprising that the growth and status of the community is often caught between two divergent narratives: on one side, there is a story of change; on the other, a story of things staying the same (or getting worse). The first story focuses on the increase in support and social recognition, the second on the shrinking avenues for political advocacy and on the absence of civil rights. Both stories are true, to a certain extent. Their seeming incompatibility stems from different understandings of what counts as meaningful change, and what counts as success from a social movement perspective.

From a sociological standpoint, the contrast between the two narratives cannot be easily reconciled with dominant theoretical explanations of sociopolitical change. The majority of academic writing on NGO advocacy operates within an understanding of change that leans heavily toward a rights-based model of political engagement that measures success in terms of structural, legislative, or policy change. In the case of sexual identity activism, for example, the recognition of same-sex unions and the presence of antidiscrimination policies based on sexual orientation and gender identity (SOGI) are often taken as a metric for the success or failure of movements (Kahlina 2015; Thoreson 2014). Even approaches that strive to move beyond conceptualizations of change in purely political, structural, and policy terms (see, for example, Banaszak and Ondercin 2016; Polletta 2008; Polletta and Jasper 2001; Tarrow 2013) tend to take activists' experiences in (Western) democracies as a starting point (Dai and Spires 2018), leading to a model heavily based on political contention as a pathway to change.

This critique is not new—and perhaps unsurprisingly, it has emerged and grown within the field of China studies. Starting in the late 2000s, scholars studying social contention in the PRC have been proposing alternative paradigms that can explain activist work in an authoritarian context without resorting to the compliance-resistance binary. In her most recent book on online mobilization, Jing Wang (2019, 39) calls this practice "nonconfrontational activism" and traces its conceptual history in work focused on "forms of social contention that routinely receive blessings or even support from the state because they occur within the official discourse of deference." Earlier conceptualizations, she notes, include the notion of "rightful resistance" (O'Brien and Li 2006), "embedded activism" (Ho and Edmonds 2008), "consultative authoritarianism" (Teets 2014), and "responsive authoritarianism" (Carnesecca 2015; Marquis and Bird 2018; Qiaoan and Teets 2020). Others have also pointed out effective discursive and framing strategies Chinese activists and NGOs employ as a way to gain legitimacy and visibility (Keech-Marx 2008) and to create a collective identity that aligns organizational goals with the notion of working for the public good (Wu 2017).

In my research, I build on this existing body of literature as I explore strategies for social change in the context of the tongzhi movement in contemporary China. The tongzhi experience is especially fitting to expose the limits of a protest-based, politically contentious model of social change. Tongzhi groups operate in an authoritarian context that prohibits public protest and heavily restricts rights-based discourse, but they also enjoy relative degrees of freedom—enabled by the central state's relative disinterest in sexual identity issues. At the same time, groups navigate a treacherous discursive field informed by the transnational circulation of models for sexual identity politics that have been developed in Western anglophone democracies and that promote "out and proud" visibility and an understanding of "LGBT rights as human rights" (Chou 2001; Thoreson 2014). While such models offer opportunities for transnational cooperation and support, their reliance on human rights discourse also makes them politically risky and difficult to sustain.

My work strives to disentangle these multiple social, cultural, and political constraints and opportunities through an analysis of tongzhi organizers' conceptualizations of, and approaches to, social change. I look at the tactical approaches that tongzhi groups have developed in order to navigate the fragmented and ambiguous political environment in which they operate, focusing particularly on their strategic use of language and discursive tactics. In so doing, I offer a way to think about social movements' political and cultural work in situations where protest and contention are not possible.

Mobilization under Authoritarian Rule: Media, State Rhetoric, and the Problem with Rights

China's economic reform at the end of the 1970s led to drastic changes in the relationship between the state and civil society. The country's modernization project involved state downsizing and the decentering of social welfare provisions, which created an opportunity for the emergence of grassroots groups and the development of relatively autonomous civil society organizations (Dai and Spires 2018; Hildebrandt 2018). Less than three decades after the beginning of the reform period, the number of civil society groups had grown to such an extent—from 400 in 1986 to 400,000 in 2006—that scholars termed the process an "associational revolution" (Teets 2013, 21; Wang and He 2004). This proliferating civil society led to increased scholarly interest in the potential for grassroots NGOs to challenge the state's power (Hsing and Lee 2009; Ma 2005; G. Yang 2005).

Discussions of the growing power of Chinese civil society reached a peak with the diffusion of information and communication technologies (ICTs) in the country, and particularly with the rapid growth of internet users (Tai 2006; G. Yang 2009; Y. Zhao 2008). While the potential democratizing effect of the internet remains under debate (Rauchfleisch and Schäfer 2015; Tsui 2003; Y. Zhao 2008; Y. Zheng 2007), the diffusion of ICTs has provided NGOs with more spaces and opportunities to organize, and this development has run parallel to a steady increase in public contention since the 1990s (O'Brien and Stern 2008; Zeng and Huang 2015). Social media platforms such as Tencent QQ (an instant messaging and micro-blogging platform launched in 1999) and Sina Weibo (a micro-blogging platform similar to Twitter, launched in 2009) have given activists easily accessible means to coordinate events, mobilize participants, and spread their messages in the public sphere (DeLuca, Brunner, and Sun 2016; Harwit 2017; Liu 2019a, 2019b; Tu 2016). These dynamics have further become salient with the launch in 2011 of WeChat, the most popular social app in the PRC as of 2021. In addition to being a platform for private interactions between users, WeChat allows groups to create public accounts that can be used to sponsor events, publish articles, promote visibility, and even collect donations. Since its launch, the app has completely overshadowed the popularity of earlier social media apps and websites due to its versatility.[4]

Faced with the growth of an increasingly informed, unruly, and connected public, the Chinese state responded by displaying an extraordinary adaptive capacity (Lei 2018, 171). This capacity emerges particularly clearly in the rhetoric adopted by the CCP leadership in the early 2000s—when the party was under the leadership of Hu Jintao—and after 2012, when Xi Jinping assumed the presidency. A comparison of the two administrations' approaches to governing civil society—relatively liberal in the case of President Hu, much more restrictive in the case of President Xi—is central to the development of strategies in the context of the tongzhi movement, as all currently active tongzhi organizations were founded in or after the early 2000s. Most groups were created during Hu Jintao's presidency and subsequently experienced the increasingly aggressive stance toward public contention that characterizes President Xi's CCP.

When a rise in domestic unrest challenged Hu's presidency at the beginning of his term, he looked for a possible solution in the concept of a "harmonious society" (和谐社会 *hexie shehui*). President Hu adopted the framework as the official party agenda in 2004, relying on the concept of social harmony to promote stability and order as the most important goals for the Chinese nation (Guo and Guo 2008; Biddulph 2015). In October 2006, during the Sixth Plenary Session of the Sixteenth Central Committee of the Communist Party of China, the country officially adopted Hu's "Resolution on Major Issues Regarding the Building of a Harmonious Socialist Society,"[5] formalizing the adoption of the harmony rhetoric as a guideline for China's future. The harmonious society discourse had clear implications for managing social unrest, and it was efficiently used to justify an increased level of media censorship and surveillance at the end of 2010, in the wake of the Arab Spring uprisings (Lei 2018, 172).[6] Despite this increased preoccupation with managing civil society and the public sphere, Hu's leadership also adopted a fairly liberal stance toward public grievances, taking steps to improve government transparency and responding to public outcry in matters of government corruption and misfeasance (Fu and Distelhorst 2017).

The ascent to power of Xi Jinping marked a turning point for state-society relationships. Under Xi's presidency, the management of dissenting public opinions and of civil society organizations has become "a question of not only social stability but also ideological struggle and national security" (Lei 2018, 172). While maintaining his predecessor's emphasis on social harmony as a prerequisite for a strong nation, President Xi adopted a new rhetorical strategy by promoting a vision he called the "Chinese Dream." The Chinese Dream refers to Xi's agenda of rejuvenating the Chinese nation, and its rhetoric emphasizes history, culture, and patriotism while aligning the national dream with issues of central importance to the general public, such as financial stability and access to public healthcare and housing (Z. Wang 2014).

The nationalist rhetoric of Xi's Chinese Dream carries important implications for grassroots NGOs and civil society organizations. The Dream's emphasis on building a strong nation underscores President Xi's concerns about the risk of an ideological dissolution of China under the attack of Western forces that, according to Xi, are conspiring to influence public opinion—particularly through the internet (Lei 2018; S. Zhao 2016). In April 2013, Xi circulated a communiqué—which would come to be known as Document 9—in which he instructed party officials to be on guard against seven "false ideological trends, positions, and activities."[7] Included in the list were, among others, Western constitutional democracy, universal human rights, civil society, neoliberalism, and notions of media independence from the party.

President Xi's administration ushered a new era of more stringent control over Chinese civil society, and Xi's narrative and directives have had important practical implications for grassroots activists in the country. In 2015, international human rights agencies registered a record-breaking number of arrests of human rights lawyers—in what some have called "the largest crackdown on lawyers since the Cultural Revolution" (Lei 2018, 185). More recently, in an effort to reduce the influence of international NGOs (INGOs) in the country, Xi's administration adopted a new law regulating the activities of overseas NGOs within China (Law of the People's Republic of China on the Administration of Activities of Overseas Nongovernmental Organizations in Mainland China). The law, which went into effect in January 2017, makes it mandatory for INGOs to register with the Ministry of Public Security before establishing an office or carrying out activities, including funding activities, in China. It further mandates that INGOs coordinate with a registered domestic Chinese organization—which is particularly relevant to domestic tongzhi organizations, as the vast majority of them are unregistered (Hildebrandt 2011).

Given the preoccupation of the Chinese state with social stability and harmony since the turn of the millennium, and particularly given the increased level of scrutiny for matters related to rights, it is relatively unsurprising that much of the literature on grassroots NGOs in China has focused on strategies for survival rather than pathways toward social change (Dai and Spires 2018). And while political conditions and a shrinking of opportunities for engagement certainly make organizational survival a primary goal for Chinese groups, such a strict focus on the mere existence of groups can be limiting. Alternative forms of political contention in the PRC move beyond survival, signaling a need to expand existing theoretical conceptualizations of pathways to change.

What Change? Social Movement Outcomes beyond the Political

It has taken a surprising amount of time for social movement theory to start engaging with questions concerning social change. Early models were more concerned with explaining the process of mobilization and participation rather than movement outcomes, partly as a consequence of considering movement participants as irrational actors whose collective behavior was fundamentally separated from rational political action (Blumer 1946; Le Bon 1896; Park 1927). Doug McAdam's political process model (1982) was an important first step toward linking protest to change; despite being conceived as "a political process model of movement *emergence*," it presented activists as politicized actors striving to gain access to the political process and endowed movements with the "capacity to reshape the broader political landscape" (McAdam, McCarthy, and Zald 1996, 13). This marked an abandonment of the earlier models of social movement development, which saw the culmination of the life cycle of a movement in either collapse or absorption in the institutional environment (Jenkins 1983, 543).

Now, analyses of the political consequences of social movements make up the vast majority of social movement literature (see Amenta et al. 2010 and Amenta and Polletta 2019 for an extensive review). In more recent decades, however, some scholars have started to move beyond a conceptualization of change in terms of policy outcome, recognizing cultural change (Davis 2002; Earl 2004; Van Dyke and Taylor 2018; Williams 2004), the normalization of collective identities (Armstrong 2002; Polletta and Jasper 2001; Taylor and Whittier 1995), the diffusion of contentious terms and discourses (Polletta 2006; Tarrow 2013; Williams 1995), and changes in public opinion (Banaszak and Ondercin 2016) as key social movement outcomes.

A focus on the cultural impact of social movements does not preclude engagement with the political consequences of cultural change. In fact, scholars proposing cultural approaches to the study of movements stress an understanding of culture, structure, and politics as interrelated spheres of social life (Polletta 2012; Van Dyke and Taylor 2018, 483). For example, recent scholarship has been paying particular attention to the cultural and political consequences of generating media attention as a way to influence public opinion and subsequently shape the public agenda (Andrews and Caren 2010; Powell, Quadlin, and Pizmony-Levy 2015). The field of empirical measurements of social change has widened to include not only policies and realignments of political power but also significant organizational changes (Clemens 1993; Meyer and Whittier 1994; Polletta 2002; Rojas 2007), the emergence and crystallization of discourses (Armstrong 2002; Snow and Benford 1988; Williams 1995), patterns of linguistic innovation (Tarrow 2013), and narratives of personal change in individuals (Jasper 1997; Munson 2009).

While this growing literature begins to provide a needed alternative to work solely focused on structural and policy outcomes, the overwhelming majority of existing research is firmly contextualized in Western democracies. As a consequence, analysis of movement pathways to cultural change frequently identify public contentious performances—such as protests, demonstrations, and strikes (Johnston 2009; Tarrow 1994;

Taylor and Van Dyke 2004; Tilly 2008; Tilly and Tarrow 2006); the diffusion of political messages and oppositional frames (Diani 1996; Kubal 1998; Oliver and Johnston 2000; Snow and Benford 1988); and lobbying through institutional channels (Arthur 2011; Rojas 2007) as common strategies successfully employed by social movements to achieve their goals. What is left out is an account of the way groups conceive and promote social change under political and cultural conditions where oppositional performances are not tolerated and where few institutional channels exist for policy advocacy—such as in the case of the PRC (Dai and Spires 2018).

Recognizing this gap in theorizations of political engagement in the PRC, scholars within the field of China studies have recently started considering alternative conceptualizations of activism in an authoritarian context. This has taken the form of work that pushes against a mere "ideology of resistance" (J. Wang 2019) and that focuses instead on the gray area of nonconfrontational tactics employed by individuals and groups during their interactions with the state. Looking at mobilization in rural China, Kevin O'Brien and Lianjiang Li (2006) have documented the strategic use of official state policy and laws by villagers oppressed by corrupt local officials and have coined the term *rightful resistance* to describe this practice. Similarly, Peter Ho and Richard Louis Edmonds (2008) have identified within the environmental movement in China a form of organizing that they term *embedded activism*— this denotes a blurring of the line between civil society and the state through the use of nonconfrontational tactics that allow "green activists [to] portray themselves as partners, rather than opponents of the central authorities" (Ho 2007, 195). Looking at cases more closely related to the focus of this book, Timothy Hildebrandt (2013) has noted how HIV organizations avoid a human rights framing in favor of a public health approach in order to affect change, and Samantha Keech-Marx (2008) has proposed analyses of discursive strategies and framing tactics as a way to understand women's groups successfully mobilizing around the issue of domestic violence.

My work contributes to this growing literature on nonconfrontational activism, suggesting a focus on linguistic and discursive strategies. To understand the possibilities for social change within an authoritarian regime that precludes avenues of direct political engagement, I build on the understanding of cultural change as a significant outcome of mobilization proposed by recent social movement scholarship. In such a context, social movements serve as creators and determinants of what Van Dyke and Taylor (2018) term *ideations*: "values and beliefs, opinions, frames, language, stories, public discourse, and collective identities" (486). Tongzhi groups pursue a political project through the production of narratives, discourses, and understandings of sexual identity that allow participants to walk the line of contention without becoming oppositional. This strategic avoidance of contentious claim-making is not merely a tool for grassroots NGO survival in an illiberal political context but also an approach that can shed light on mechanisms for social change that contrast with rights-based, policy-oriented models.

The analytical focus of the book centers particularly on tongzhi narratives, language, and identity, and their interaction with—and contributions to—processes of social change. A key argument I make in this book is that discursive flexibility allows grassroot NGOs to engage in a constant process of tactical innovation and adaptation, responding to the shifting political environment and to the challenges of a government known for its capacity to learn, experiment, and adapt to changing social and political conditions (Heilmann and Perry 2011; Lei 2018). Tongzhi groups not only engage in discursive practices that maximize their chances of gaining positive visibility without overstepping the boundaries of contention but also adapt when reacting to tactical missteps or when the boundaries suddenly shift. This focus expands on the work of scholars who have pointed to language as a venue to overcome some of the limitations of framing approaches developed to explain mobilization in Western democracies—looking, for example, at adaptive strategies that rely on linguistic ambiguity (Thornton 2002).

Challenging Dichotomies: Sexual Identities in a Transnational Context

Language and narratives are central in meaning-making processes as well as the creation of collective identities (Polletta and Jasper 2001; Taylor and Whittier 1995). Studying sexual identities involves, almost by definition, linguistic work. And in the context of the "non-West," the creation of vocabularies denoting a collective identity involves negotiation and adaptation as well as inevitable confrontations with the binaries of authentic and colonial, global and local, modern and traditional (Grewal and Kaplan 2001; Leap and Boellstorff 2004; Rofel 2007; Savci 2021).

There is a growing body of scholarship that explicitly calls into question these binaries and that draws critical attention to the pitfalls of an early polarization within the field of global queer studies, which for a time was split between theories of "Western homogenization" and arguments of "local essentialism" (Zheng 2015, 10). Proponents of a homogenizing perspective placed the evolution of sexual identity and sexual identity politics on a continuum and theorized a progressive movement from repression to liberalization—the latter being represented by certain models of sexual freedom envisioned in specific Western contexts (Altman 1996, 1997; Murray 1992). Partly in response to these perspectives, subsequent works started emphasizing the distinctiveness of local sexual identities, and the work of local sexual minority groups to appropriate and "make local" foreign identities (Johnson, Jackson, and Herdt 2000; Lim 2008).

Although effective in countering a "narrowly conceived model of Americanization" (Chao 2000, 383), works decentering Western queerness are often structured in a way that juxtaposes Western anglophone modes of gayness and queerness to local and "traditional" modes (Chou 2001; T. Zheng 2015). In a way, by theorizing sexuality in non-Western contexts as fully "other," these works are limited in the same way as those depicting the emergence of sexual identity and politics as an early step in an inevitable progression: both inevitably risk reducing culture to something "timeless, bounded, homogenous, and unchanging [that] only a radical imposition of modernity from the outside seems to change" (Rofel 2007, 91–92). A partial step away from this monolithic view of culture is evidenced by research that exposes processes of hybridization, in which same-sex practices in non-Western cultures are shown to blur the line between West and non-West (Carrillo 1999; Chao 2000; Chong 2001). Still, even the hybridization perspective ends up assuming the a priori existence of Western and non-Western sexual identities that can be combined (Oswin 2004, 784).

In lieu of polarizing views that juxtapose West and non-West, global and local, modern and traditional, scholars have been calling for theoretical frameworks that move beyond paradigms of sameness or difference (Manderson and Jolly 1997) and that "probe further the relationship between globalization and culture" (Grewal and Kaplan 2001, 663). A first step consists in a shift in terminology: rather than relying on a rhetoric of globality, scholars have argued that the term *transnational* might be more helpful in capturing the complexity of sexual identities across the globe (Grewal and Kaplan 2001; Liu and Rofel 2010; Rofel 2007). A transnational approach avoids the pitfall of identifying the global with the West, as well as with a threatening force potentially endangering for the local (Oswin 2004, 785).

Necessary to an understanding of the working mechanics of this transnational dynamic process of identity-making is a focus on narratives and sexual identity discourses to challenge these binary distinctions by exposing their limits in the face of the polysemy and ambiguity of language and identity labels (Lim 2008; Sinnott 2012; Campbell-Kibler et al. 2002). The present study moves beyond a conceptualization of identities as relatively stable (or stably evolving) categories, emphasizing instead the ambiguity, flexibility, and even outright paradoxes perpetuated through narrative and linguistic creativity. In so doing, the work responds to scholarly calls for projects grounded in transnational queer sociology, following in particular Travis Kong's suggestion for analyses which "engage sociology with queer theory and highlight the importance of both material or structural and textual or discursive analyses" (Kong 2020, 6).

Lastly, my work joins recent and growing conversations on sexual identities, queer representation, and queer political mobilization in East Asia and in the Sinophone world in particular. Scholars in anthropology, Asian studies, sexuality studies, and cultural and media studies have extensively analyzed queer cultures and identities in the PRC, Hong Kong, and Taiwan (Bao 2020; Brainer 2019; Chiang and Heinrich 2014; Chou 2000; Engebretsen 2014; Kam 2013; Rofel 2007; Yue and Leung 2017, just to cite a few). Among these, Hongwei Bao (2018, 25, emphasis in original) points out the need for analytical focus toward "the *political* implications of *tongzhi* identity and activism for contemporary social movements and radical politics." A focus on tongzhi strategies for change contributes to social movement literature by calling into question a model for social change that relies on confrontational tactics, protest, and political contention. Mobilizing work on transnational queer activism, this book will also discuss the limits of rights-based approaches to tongzhi organizing in the context of transnational cooperation. In the political context of contemporary China, tongzhi groups are increasingly seeking to distance themselves from international organizations who heavily rely on the language of human rights. To make cooperation possible, groups creatively engage in processes of translation and adaptation that allow them to downplay the most contentious elements of transnational rights discourses.

Ultimately, this book explores an alternative model for political organizing that explains change in the absence of protest through an emphasis on discursive strategies and, particularly, on the interactive and dialogical practices of cultural and discursive production. The model outlined in this book brings to communication social movement theory and transnational queer studies a focus on discursive and linguistic processes as a way to problematize Western, right-based approaches to sexual identity mobilization and visibility.

Project Overview

At the onset of this research, I was broadly interested in understanding the way tongzhi groups conceptualize their work—and perhaps their project for change—in the social and political context of the PRC. As I became more familiar with the work of various groups, I was struck by the linguistic and rhetorical dynamism characterizing the community. The way organizers were paying attention to what tongzhi groups were saying, when they were saying it, and how it was said pointed me toward language and discourse as a key element that needed to be unpacked. I started seeing groups' rhetorical work as more than a strategic tool for organizational survival and as something closer to an interactive mechanism through which tongzhi organizers were making sense and acting upon the social, cultural, and political forces shaping their environment.

To untangle the dynamic interactions in which tongzhi groups engage to promote their project of change, I relied on a combination of ethnographic fieldwork, semistructured interviews and conversations, and discourse analysis of online and offline media. I collected data between 2016 and 2019, gathering the majority of ethnographic and interview data during six months of fieldwork conducted in 2016 and 2017. In a preliminary research phase, I participated in events and had informal meetings with tongzhi in six cities (Beijing, Nanjing, Shanghai, Hangzhou, Guangzhou, and Xi'an), but I ultimately decided to limit my field sites to the three urban centers of Beijing, Shanghai, and Guangzhou. I chose these three cities partly due to their national, political, and cultural importance: Beijing is the capital and the political heart of the PRC, as it houses the central headquarters for the CCP and the State Council; Shanghai is the country's global financial and technological core; and Guangzhou is a hub for intellectual and commercial innovation and exchange, due to its location bordering the South China Sea and being geographically close to Hong Kong. These three cities are also the locations with the highest concentration of tongzhi groups and activities in the PRC, and they house the headquarters of all the largest and most influential tongzhi groups. These are groups that work on a national scale, with regional and local chapters in multiple provinces, and whose online and offline work significantly influences and shapes the tongzhi community at large.

I conducted the majority of my participant observations at events organized by some of these groups, attending a total of twenty-four weekly events and activities. A particularly key event was the tenth anniversary of a "national conference" organized by the largest tongzhi group in the PRC, PFLAG China. As I detail in Chapter 3, to celebrate the anniversary, the group decided to organize their annual meeting on a cruise ship traveling from Shanghai to Fukuoka (Japan), a four-day trip packed with activities and culminating in the first symbolic collective same-sex wedding organized by a tongzhi group. Other events included workshops, structured discussions, film screenings, expert debates, museum exhibits, and more. Events were almost always interactive, and attending them allowed me to observe exchanges and debates on a wide variety of topics—from coming out stories to strategic approaches to visibility, from past achievements to future goals.

I complemented my ethnographic work with in-person interviews. Between August and September 2017, I collected interview data from a total of 107 individuals. The majority of the individuals I interviewed (74 percent) identified as members of the tongzhi community, and the remaining participants were actively involved in community events as either parents of tongzhi (23 percent) or as teachers who had participated in training workshops offered by tongzhi groups (3 percent). Almost half (44 percent) of the tongzhi I interviewed were involved in group activities in some organizational capacity—as event organizers, group leaders, or volunteers. All participants were Chinese nationals, and the vast majority of the interviews (92 percent) was conducted in Chinese (Putonghua). I mostly relied on in-person recruitment methods, introducing myself as a researcher at the beginning of events and inviting attendees to approach me if they were interested in chatting. My presence as a foreign researcher at tongzhi events rarely went unnoticed, and introducing myself in Chinese while identifying as "an Italian *lala*" simultaneously generated interest and signaled my cultural knowledge of the community.

Interview data comes from a combination of formal, semistructured in-depth interviews—which were recorded and transcribed—and hundreds of informal, semistructured and unstructured conversations, which were not audio recorded and for which I relied on memory, written notes, and voice memos recorded immediately after each conversation. I conducted informal conversations with all 107 study participants, and I formally interviewed 52 of them. As I explain in more detail in the methodological appendix, informal conversations often yielded more useful, rich data than formal interviews, as the absence of an audio recorder between me and my participants made the interaction more natural and markedly improved rapport. In both interviews and conversations, I allowed the conversation to develop organically and embraced the possibility of the discussion moving in unexpected and unplanned directions. At the same time, I prepared and memorized a topic guide that I could rely on to keep the momentum going or to bring the conversation back to issues concerning change. The topic guide included issues concerning identity and self, involvement with tongzhi groups, changes in the social and political environment of the PRC, the current work and future hopes of tongzhi groups, and the perception of sexual identity movements outside of the PRC. I constantly updated this guide throughout my time in the field, for example adding questions on specific events

Figure I.1 Cities and Number of Study Participants. (*Adapted from https://d-maps .com/carte.php?num_car=17501&lang=en. © 2022 https://d-maps.com.*)

that had recently happened or incorporating topics that I noticed were being discussed online by members of the community.

I use pseudonyms throughout the book to protect the identity of participants, with a few exceptions. Some organizers are well-known public figures due to their central position in their organization, and they authorized me (and sometimes explicitly requested) to use the pseudonyms they are publicly known by. This is the case, for example, of PFLAG executive director Ah Qiang, Tongyu director Xian, and Quancuhui founder Yanzi. For all other study participants I mention the tongzhi groups with which they are affiliated, but I refer to the participants with pseudonyms. Most tongzhi use nicknames—often in the form of references to nature—as pseudonyms for interactions within the community, so I mirrored this practice in my naming choices and assigned names of animals, plants, minerals, and other natural elements.

Lastly, I supplemented my ethnographic fieldwork and interviews with a discursive and content analysis of online materials. I systematically collected tongzhi groups' WeChat and Weibo publications while in the field and subsequently coded and analyzed a small subset of them—coding a total of 157 articles and publications. I consider groups' publications on their official WeChat accounts a vital part of the discursive and rhetorical repertoires employed by groups, and I paid particular attention to dialogical processes of meaning construction. I compared my observations at tongzhi events to the official accounts that groups gave of such events in subsequent publications, and when possible, I compared groups' publications to local and international newspaper articles dealing with tongzhi issues and activities. This allowed me to compare discourses across multiple media and to examine the cultural and symbolic struggles tongzhi organizers engaged in as they defined issues, goals, aspirations, and ideas (Davis 2002; Kane 1997; Steinberg 1998).

Combining these multiple sources of data made it possible for me to access different discursive spaces and practices with which tongzhi groups engage and the strategies they mobilize. By following and analyzing the interactions across different media and data sources, I strived to untangle some of the complexity characterizing the discursive environment of tongzhi advocacy in the PRC, uncovering groups' conceptualizations of and strategies for social change.

It is important to note that while I often use the shorthand "tongzhi groups" and "tongzhi organizing" in my analysis, I do not mean to suggest that the kind of organizing I discuss is the only kind of sexual identity activism happening in the PRC. The focus of this research is necessarily limited to organizations that were active while I was in the field and that I observed as being particularly successful at navigating tightening conditions for grassroots organizing. In fact, it was precisely their successes compared to other groups that helped me crystallize the central puzzle of this book around noncontentious strategies. When my research was in its early stages, it incorporated forms of activism that more explicitly pushed the limits of confrontation—in particular, I had been following lala organizations that aligned themselves closely with feminist groups (including members of the Feminist Five, a group of young women who were arrested in Beijing in March 2015 after staging a protest against sexual harassment on public transit). However, I made the decision to move away from an analysis of these groups when, while in the field, it became clear that activists were under serious threat. During the summer of 2017, in the midst of my fieldwork, a wave of governmental crackdowns resulted in feminist groups experiencing increased surveillance and harassment. Groups had to drastically reduce activities and in many cases stop them altogether. In some cases, including a conversation I initiated with one of the Feminist Five, participants stated they did not want interviews included in published work. I initially took my distance from targeted groups to protect my participants, and as research progressed, I made the conscious choice to focus my analysis on other organizations that were adopting strategies for change that allowed them to avoid crackdowns such as those experienced by these feminist groups.

Chapter Overview

This book begins by historically locating the emergence of nonnormative sexual identities and political discourses in modern China. Chapter 1 traces the development of identity labels by looking at the transnational history of language and terminology used to describe same-sex behavior, including the emergence of a political tongzhi identity in postsocialist China. As tongzhi groups grew in visibility and political engagement, they experienced changes in political opportunities, the emergence of transnational networks of ideas and information exchange, and the diffusion of new communication technologies.

Chapter 2 focuses on the largest tongzhi group currently active in China, PFLAG China (Tongxinglian Qinyouhui), exploring how the language of the family is strategically employed to emphasize family belonging over sexual identity. PFLAG organizers strategically rely on culturally salient discourses to transform the meaning of tradition in ways that allow them to simultaneously align their work with "traditional values" and with a political project of change. This chapter discusses the narrative strategy of sharing "coming home" stories—that is, stories told by parents of young tongzhi who have come out to them— and analyzes the group's reliance on the language of social harmony as a discursive tactic to advance the tongzhi project of social and political belonging.

Chapter 3 compares two events organized by PFLAG in May and June 2017, respectively: the unsuccessful "520" event, in which a group of mothers of tongzhi were forcibly removed from Shanghai's "marriage market" in Renmin Park, and the successful "marriage cruise," the first collective same-sex wedding organized by a tongzhi organization in China. The comparison allows an analysis of the conditions under which the group is effective in lowering the perceived political contentiousness of activities and the circumstances under which it fails. The analysis focuses on the way organizers experiment, learn from their mistakes and successes, and adapt their tactics and discourses based on the results. I particularly emphasize discursive flexibility and adaptation in the form of alignment with state discourses and the downplaying of the political as a strategy to achieve positive visibility in the public sphere.

Chapter 4 introduces a strategy for change that moves beyond a rhetoric of harmony and belonging by selectively mobilizing the language of rights. In a number of recent lawsuits, tongzhi plaintiffs have sought legal resolutions of cases regarding forced conversion therapy, stigmatizing information in college textbooks, media censorship, and workplace discrimination. This chapter analyzes the discursive and linguistic work tongzhi groups, individual plaintiffs, and their lawyers engaged in to maximize their chances in the courtroom and follows the transnational diffusion of news of the events. There are notable discrepancies between international coverage—mostly focused on rights and policy change—and tongzhi groups' understandings of the cases as opportunities to influence public opinion and explore the limits of the language of human rights in the context of transnational cooperation.

1

Tongzhi, Lala, Deviants, and Queers

Legacies and Politics of Sexual Identity Language

In July 2017, one of my tongzhi friends in Guangzhou invited me to an event held in Puning, a county-level city in the southeast of Guangdong province. The event promised to be a break from the activities in large urban centers I had been attending up to that point, so I enthusiastically agreed.[1] Halfway through the event, all participants moved to a nearby restaurant for lunch, and I sat at a small table with three young tongzhi—Plover, Mallard, and Teal, aged twenty-two to twenty-five—and an older tongzhi, thirty-six-year-old Scoter.[2] As we were waiting for food to be served, the following conversation unfolded at our table:

> PLOVER: There are mostly gays and lesbians at this event.
> MALLARD: Oh, but I think that person that was on stage before may be trans.
> PLOVER: Yeah, you are right. So there are also trans.
> TEAL: But there are no queers.
> SCOTER: What is a queer?
> TEAL: A queer is someone who used to be homosexual but now is also other things. So perhaps they also like the opposite sex.
> SCOTER [*confused*]: But isn't that a bisexual?

TEAL: Yes. No. Well, queer is different. It can be both. Queer is a bit of everything.

PLOVER: But there are no queers here. Except maybe her [*pointing at me*]. She comes from Milan, Italy! [*Laughs.*]

Plover's final line is a play on the Chinese character 酷 *ku*, which makes up the first part of 酷儿 *ku'er* (queer) but also means cool, fashionable, and stylish. The joke is multilayered—on one side, identifying me as a potential ku'er played on the fact that Milan is a well-known fashion hub and a coveted shopping destination for people looking for high-end designer clothes. On the other side, contrasting my potential queerness with the absence of queers at the event had much to do with my positionality as a foreigner and as a researcher from a university in the United States as well as with our location in Puning, geographically removed from large southern urban centers like Guangzhou. Scoter's confusion is understandable—as an identity term, *queer* in contemporary China is not widespread. It is commonly associated with the young urban elite, and the term has been appropriated by some (usually young, female, urban, and Western-educated) groups as a political identity. It is a term that explicitly questions the traditional boundaries of national belonging, as it is a phonetic transliteration of a foreign term rather than a translation.

The exchange at our lunch table in Puning was spontaneous and lighthearted, but it exposed key tensions I had been tracing in my months in the field. For marginalized groups fighting for recognition, labels hold particular significance, and their meanings and uses can inform the shape, visibility, and political import of the community. Just as ku'er is coded as urban and transnational, identity terms circulating in the contemporary tongzhi community hold multiple meanings whose historical legacy is often made salient in subtle and strategic ways across various contexts. The history of the tongzhi community is intimately intertwined with the history of the language used to define, identify, and mobilize the community itself.

In this chapter, I trace the emergence of sexual identities and political discourses of sexuality in the PRC, and I discuss the development of various identity labels and their tensions. To do so, I look at the transnational history of the language connected to same-sex behavior and (later) to nonnormative sexual identities. I follow linguistic changes in the context of transformations in the sociopolitical environment of postsocialist China, and I present the growth in political visibility of the community as a consequence of changing political opportunities, transnational networks, and new communication technologies—all of which facilitated the diffusion of tongzhi discourses and vocabularies.

From Practice to Perversion: The "Emergence" of Homosexuality in China

The first appearance of the terms *tongxinglian* and *tongxing'ai* (both meaning "same-sex love") can be traced to the beginning of the twentieth century (T. Zheng 2015), though same-sex desire existed and was documented long before then. Historians and literary scholars have amply documented the history of (mostly male) homoeroticism in imperial China, tracing the frequent use of poetic and evocative metaphors used to describe same-sex behavior. Some of the most common and widely cited metaphors include the "passion of the cut sleeve" (*duan xiu zhi pi*), the "bitten peach" (*fen tao*), and "allied brothers" (*xianghuo xiongdi*) (Chou 2000; W. Wei 2007, 574). Classical Chinese, as a language, lacked a term to identify a person attracted to someone of the same sex (T. Zheng 2015, 34), and metaphors such as those listed here strictly hinted at a behavior but carried no identity connotations for those who engaged in it (Chou 2001; Hinsch 2002). Sexual behavior between men was acknowledged and tolerated as long as men respected their social role and their family obligations of getting married and having children (Cao and Lu 2014; Kang 2009; Kong 2016). Sexual behavior between women constituted even less of an issue, as it was considered "negligible and insignificant" (Kong 2016, 498) since it did not undermine patriarchal relations of power within the family.

In the late nineteenth and early twentieth centuries, amid the political turmoil and national crisis following defeat in the Sino-Japanese War of 1894, China started a grand modernization project as a way to protect the country from the threat of imperialism (D. Zhao 2001, 56). The project included the introduction of numerous Western social theories in China, a trend that continued after the Republican Revolution in 1911. It was in this context that Chinese intellectuals started to apply a scientific approach to the study of sexual behavior, strongly influenced by Western sexology and the writings of Havelock Ellis, Magnus Hirschfeld, Edward Carpenter, and Sigmund Freud. Prominent intellectuals such as Zhang Jingsheng and Pan Guangdan—the latter a famous Chinese eugenicist with degrees from Dartmouth and Columbia—translated Western scientific texts on the subject and introduced *tongxinglian*[3] as a medical term to identify a type of deviant sexual behavior (Chiang 2010; Chou 2000; Kong 2016).

The medicalization of sexual practices contributed to the emergence of a definition of homosexuality as pathological deviance from the norm (Kang 2009), and under the influence of Freudian psychoanalysis, the prerepublican-era cultural understanding of same-sex desire was replaced by the scientific category of homosexuality as a type of sexual perversion (Chiang 2010, 644). When Zhang Jingsheng published *Sex Histories* in 1926—a collection of seven life histories that he collected and psychoanalyzed—he briefly addressed same-sex behavior between men, calling anal sex "perverted, malodorous, meaningless, and inhumane behavior" (Zhang 1926, cited in Chiang 2010, 636–37). Importantly, in the political context of Republican China, intellectuals reframed homosexuality as a symptom of national weakness and backwardness. This pathologizing of same-sex desire meant that those engaging in such behavior were singled out by media, intellectuals, and the ruling elite as abnormal and morally deplorable, as "what was once an emblem of aesthetic culture and social status was transformed into a reprehensible and disgraceful practice that came to be seen as one of many causes of a weak nation" (T. Zheng 2015, 39).

The discussion and regulation of sexual behavior underwent another dramatic shift with the end of the republic and the establishment of the People's Republic of China in 1949. Mao's social reforms and the switch to a planned economy led to new forms of social organization—the commune system in the countryside and the *danwei* (work-unit) system in urban areas—which effectively brought individuals' public and private lives under direct state control. The systems almost completely erased privacy, especially in urban areas, where "any breach or propriety or morality was likely to come to the attention of [the danwei] leaders" (Ho et al. 2018, 488). During the Maoist era, heterosexual sex in marriage for the purpose of reproduction became the only type of acceptable sexual practice, as the state considered all other kinds of sex a distraction from the revolutionary project and needed workers' bodies and their reproductive abilities to create the next generation of workers (Honig 2003; T. Zheng 2009).

While homosexual practices were never rendered illegal from a strictly legislative standpoint, consensual same-sex acts were morally and socially condemned, and those who engaged in them were often punished for their behavior. This was exacerbated during the Cultural Revolution (1966–76), when sodomy[4] was heavily policed as a deviant product of capitalism and those practicing it were marked by the Red Guards as "bad elements" to be punished (Cao and Lu 2014; Geyer 2002). Men caught engaging in sexual acts with one another faced public humiliation and arrest and were often punished with imprisonment or forced labor in camps and detention centers (Worth et al. 2017). In my conversations with older tongzhi who had lived through the Cultural Revolution, they often spoke of those years as—in retrospect—responsible for their difficulties in coming to terms with their sexual orientation. One day I was strolling through the streets of Guangzhou with Creek, a male tongzhi born in 1954 whom I had first met in Shanghai a few months prior. His white hair and gentle smile had become a familiar presence at many tongzhi events, which he often joined as an unofficial photographer. That day, Creek invited me to his apartment for tea—a welcome respite from the humid heat of the city—and as we sat down, he reminisced about his first exposure to homosexuality as a concept during the late 1960s and early '70s. He explained to me that he resisted acknowledging his attraction to men for a long time because of his memory of those years:

> During the Cultural Revolution I would hear people say, or sometimes I even saw the posters outside of courts, I saw that someone had committed a crime, something bad like the crime of sodomy, or . . . although it was seldom, but sometimes when I read newspaper reports, or things like that, or when people talked about these things, all the message I got was very negative. So although I didn't have a very clear understanding of

homosexuality, I had the impression that it was something . . . not good.

Creek's experience was one shared by many tongzhi of his generation, many of whom entered heterosexual marriages and never became part of the tongzhi community for fear of repercussions for themselves and for their family.[5]

The devastating effect that Mao's social and economic policies had on Chinese society—the Cultural Revolution being just one of the most well-known examples—paved the way for economic reform at the end of the 1970s. The new wave of reform marked the beginning of what scholars have gone so far as to term a "sexual revolution" for China and represented a turning point for the emergence of a Chinese homosexual community. For the first time in the history of the PRC, homosexuality emerged as a sexual *identity*, as those engaging in same-sex behavior started linking their sexual practices to a particular sexual subjectivity—identifying for the first time as homosexuals.

China's "Sexual Revolution" and the Development of a Tongzhi Identity

After Mao's death in 1976, the PRC underwent another period of vast socioeconomic transformations. Faced with increasing grievances from the population, a collapsing economy, and widespread social crisis, China's new leaders implemented economic policies that opened the country's doors to the world. Sexuality scholars often identify the social transformation following Deng Xiaoping's 1978 economic reform as a key moment for the emergence of new sexual subjectivities, fueled by a relaxation of state control over individual lives and by an increased volume of intellectual exchange with outsiders (Ho et al. 2018; Rofel 1999, 2007; D. Wong 2016).

The reform period was one characterized by contradictions. Deng's open-door policy welcomed an influx of foreign ideas, but it would be shortsighted to characterize its effects merely as a "Westernization" of the country. In fact, at the same time China experienced a strong revival of some of its oldest tradition, particularly Confucianism and neo-

Confucianism (D. Zhao 2001, 50), and the state carried out police campaigns designed to punish behaviors deemed "too Western" (M. Tanner 2000). Despite the relaxation of state control over individual lives, new kinds of policing and social control emerged in the form of restrictive demographic policies, a neoliberal governmentality that exacerbated inequalities (particularly across rural/urban lines), and technology-mediated state control over freedom of expression.

For the nascent tongzhi community, a significant social outcome of the economic reform concerned a change in the relationship between individuals and their families of origin. Changing social dynamics led to a simultaneous increase of constraints and freedoms, particularly in the context of parental pressures. In 1979, the introduction of the one-child policy created a generation of children who were living with the pressure of being solely responsible for the continuation of the family lineage. For young tongzhi born after 1979, having no siblings meant living with the burden of being their parents "only hope" (Fong 2004) while feeling unable to fulfill their parents' expectations. Many gave in to parental pressure, to the point that the neologism 同妻 *tongqi*[6] was coined in the early 2000s to identify heterosexual women who had unknowingly married a male tongzhi. And although there is no equivalent neologism to describe a heterosexual male married to a female tongzhi, in a patriarchal society like China young women with no siblings often have very few economic alternatives to marriage. Ivy, a twenty-four-year-old lala from a city south of Shanghai, described to me the situation of two of her female friends and the pressures that had led them there:

> I know two friends, both were forced to marry and they were only children, so there was no way to compromise. They got married, gave birth to a child, and now they live in pain, these lala, but they had no other way. I feel Chinese mothers can be a little . . . have you heard the expression 寻死觅活 [*xunsi mihuo*, "clutching their pearls" / "threatening suicide to express pain and disappointment"]? . . . Many moms will say things, they will tell you "if you don't get married, I will die. I will die with you, let us die." They will cry and cry, and stop eating, and ask why their child is doing that to them, a lot of this. And the family will be broken.

Ivy connected the idea of her friends being only children to having no leverage at all when it came to their choice of marrying a man. In her view, the option of expressing a desire to remain unwed was too risky for her friends, as it would ultimately threaten the stability and integrity of the family lineage. This was a common worry of tongzhi and lala in their late twenties and early thirties I spoke with who were not out to their parents. Most of them feared they would soon have to face a choice—give in to parental pressure and enter an unhappy marriage or risk jeopardizing family stability and parental happiness.

At the same time, the reform era led to a new geographic mobility through a restructuring of the Mao-era *hukou* (household registration) system, which had been created to avoid migration to the cities. Under Deng Xiaoping, the system was altered to allow temporary migration for work or study purposes, leading to the relaxation of the strict division between the urban and rural population and allowing for an increased physical distance between generations within the family system—which also meant a rise in freedom and autonomy for the younger generation (Ho et al. 2018). Participants in my study who had experienced the reform period as young adults often talked about the potential for anonymity offered by large metropoles removed from their hometown. Naga, the forty-one-year-old founder of one of the first lala groups in Shanghai, described her reasons for moving to the city in these terms:

> [My girlfriend and I] liked Shanghai very much. Because Shanghai. . . . In those years, we all saw relatively large cities like Shanghai and Beijing and we thought: "Maybe we should go there, where no one knows us." So we moved to those places. Living in the big cities, we felt there was no pressure. That was the idea at the time. Because there were no relatives, no classmates in the city.

Naga's recollection points to the newfound freedom Chinese youth were experiencing as a consequence of new geographic possibilities, and emphasizes the potential for unprecedented independence from family scrutiny. Furthermore, the 1979 one-child policy contributed to the geographic separation, as it led to a generation of only children on whom parents invested an unprecedented amount of resources—including investing larger sums of money in their education in order to send them to prestigious universities in large urban centers.

Yet another somewhat contradictory and unintended effect of the one-child policy affected the realm of sexuality and sexual behavior, as the implementation of the policy contributed to the separation of sex from procreation (Ho et al. 2018, 490). This removed the stigma associated with nonreproductive sex that had characterized the Cultural Revolution—when excessive and deviant sex had been identified as a product of capitalism (Cao and Lu 2014). Together with increased mobility, economic growth, and technological development, changes in understandings of sex led to an emergence of a new sensibility, one that Lisa Rofel (2007) characterized as the emergence of "desiring subjects." A new generation of tongzhi started coming of age in the postreform era, with no memory of life under Mao. This generation began to pursue personal desires through travel, exchange, consumption, and pleasure— including sexual pleasure.

The dramatic change in social attitudes toward sex and desire was reflected in linguistic practices within the tongzhi community—in fact, the 1990s was the first decade in which individuals started relying on tongxinglian as an identity label. Scholars have documented linguistic changes that show the shift from an understanding of homosexuality as a behavior to the creation of an identity based on sexual preference: in the words of those engaging in same-sex behavior in the '90s, homosexuality stopped being something a person *does* (我搞同性恋 *wo gao tongxinglian* "I play with homosexuality") and became something one *is* (我是同性恋 *wo shi tongxinglian* "I am homosexual") (Chou 2001). This change marked the first time that *tongxinglian* was appropriated by members of the community as an identity detached from the negative, pathologized, socially deviant connotations of the 1920s and instead signifying belonging to a particular community.

The conceptual shift from behavior to identity also led to the emergence of new identity labels as an alternative to the medical-sounding *tongxinglian*. In the mid-1990s, the term *tongzhi* started circulating among members of the community. The term itself embodies and symbolizes the cultural and transnational dynamics that characterize the emergence of tongzhi groups in the PRC: its literal meaning is "common will," and its history carries clear revolutionary undertones—its first use in a political context is attributed to Sun Yat-Sen, who used it to refer to his followers during the revolution he led against the late Qing dynasty at the beginning of the twentieth century, and the term was later chosen by the CCP to translate the word *comrade* from Russian (Kong, Lau, and Hui 2019; Wong 2005). There are multiple accounts of how *tongzhi* came to be reclaimed to signify same-sexual identities (Wong 2005), but most scholars identify the pivotal year as 1989, when Hong Kong playwright Edward Lam used the term for the Chinese title of the first Hong Kong Lesbian and Gay Film Festival—which he dubbed Hong Kong Tongzhi Film Festival (Bao 2018; Leung 2008). The term quickly became popular in Hong Kong and shortly thereafter in Taiwan, where its use to encompass nonnormative sexualities and sexual orientations further crystalized in 1992, when Lam used it to translate a section of the Taipei Golden Horse International Film Festival titled "New Queer Cinema" (Kong, Lau, and Hui 2019; Leung 2008). *Tongzhi* then spread to the PRC in the mid-1990s, its diffusion strongly fueled by the first Hong Kong Tongzhi Conference held in 1996, shortly before the official return of the island to the PRC the following year.

The appropriation of *tongzhi* as a sexual identity term shares some similarities with the reclaiming of *queer* by individuals and groups in the United States. Yet while U.S. queers were taking control of a term historically used to discriminate against their community, tongzhi appropriated a term that had historically signified inclusion, as a marker of cultural and political belonging. At the same time, the adoption of *tongzhi* was also a political provocation, as that was—and still is—the term used among members of the CCP to address each other. Helen Leung (2008, 3) notes that *tongzhi* "shares the appropriative and irreverent spirit of queer" as a consciously unruly take on a serious political term. For Hong Kong activists in the 1990s, reliance on *tongzhi* instead of *gay/lesbian* or LGBT was also a conscious move on the part of tongzhi community leaders and organizers to distance their efforts from a Western approach to sexual identity politics (Wong 2004). The distancing was made explicit in one of the main points in the manifesto of the 1996 Hong Kong conference:

> The les-bi-gay movement in many Western societies is largely built upon the notion of individualism, confrontational politics,

and the discourse of individual rights. Certain characteristics of confrontational politics, such as "coming out," mass protests, and parades may not be the best way of achieving tongzhi liberation in the family-centered, community-oriented Chinese societies, which stress the importance of social harmony. In formulating the tongzhi movement strategy, we should take the specific socio-economic and cultural environment of each society into consideration.[7]

The use of *tongzhi* as a marker for cultural authenticity and political belonging (Wong 2004) highlights a key tension embedded in the political use of the term: it invokes the voice and legacy of Chinese revolutionaries while simultaneously signifying explicit opposition to the confrontational tactics of Western sexual identity activism. This tension is a productive one—as an identity term, *tongzhi* provided a sense of community, collective belonging, and political possibility within the confines of strict state control. While the manifesto undoubtedly essentialized both Chinese and Western (Anglo-Saxon) culture, it also paved the road for models of community organizing that could exist even in an authoritarian context that strongly limited opportunities for political engagement. This was particularly important for members of the tongzhi community in the PRC, who were faced with a political environment where—despite the fundamental changes the reform period brought to approaches to sex and sexuality—state regulation of sexual behavior remained deeply conservative for the first twenty years after the implementation of Deng's open-door policy. This conservative stance manifested clearly in the medical, legal, and social definitions of homosexuality and same-sex behavior.

Tongzhi in the PRC had to contend with social understandings of homosexuality as a pathological, deviant behavior. The first version of the *Chinese Classification of Mental Disorders* (*CCMD*) in 1979 listed homosexuality as a sexual disorder, and homosexual acts—while not criminalized—were often punished under the charge of "hooliganism" (*liumangzui*), a broadly defined offense introduced in 1979 and designed to encompass all those activities perceived as a danger to the social order (H. Tanner 2000). Four years after the introduction of the crime of hooliganism, in 1983, the Chinese state launched its first Strike Hard (*yanda*) campaign, also known as an Anti Spiritual Pollution campaign. The campaign specifically targeted attitudes deemed too liberal, bourgeois, and Western and resulted in the violent punishment of any behavior deemed immoral, obscene, or too individualistic (M. Tanner 2000). This social and legal context, paired with the political sensitivity of social gatherings in the aftermath of Tiananmen in 1989, made tongzhi organizing in the PRC virtually impossible until the late 1990s.

The Beginning of Tongzhi Community Activism

For the first two decades postreform, the tongzhi community stayed largely invisible and removed from the political arena. According to medical and legal definitions, homosexuality oscillated between being a mental illness and a deviant behavior, and members of the nascent community could only meet in secret, often at late-night gatherings in urban parks and spas. Information about the meetings was passed along via word of mouth—and even then, details were kept to a minimum. Creek, the older tongzhi who had lived through the Cultural Revolution, told me of the hours he had spent riding his bike in circles around the Forbidden City in search of a meeting place he had heard about: "I was just riding around, because I didn't know [where the meeting place was], so . . . and then by accident, I met a young man who became my first lover."

The secrecy was well justified, as parks and public bathrooms were common targets for police raids. So much so, in fact, that they became the subject of the first homosexual movie filmed in the PRC, Zhang Yuan's *East Palace, West Palace*. The movie, whose title is Beijing tongzhi slang for the public bathroom located on either side of the Forbidden City, was shot in 1996 but could not be released in the PRC. It premiered at the Mar del Plata Film Festival in Argentina at the end of the year but gained international popularity the following year when it was screened at the 1997 Cannes Film Festival. Its timing and transnational path toward release are significant because they are representative of fundamental changes that affected the *tongzhi* community at the time: the creation of the first tongzhi movie marks the moment, at the end of the 1990s, when multiple transnational and local forces and events converged to push the hidden tongzhi community into the political arena.

Most of the organizers I met in Beijing, Shanghai, and Guangzhou unanimously referenced 1997 as a key date for an opening up of political opportunities for groups, as that is the year hooliganism was deleted from the Chinese criminal code. Despite the fact that the hooliganism offense was never explicitly designed to punish homosexuality, for many tongzhi its abolishment marks the de facto "legalization of homosexuality" in the PRC and the beginning of political organizing in urban areas.[8] Of course, community events were taking place even in the years before 1997, including instances of political activism such as the 1996 "Beijing birthday party"—a celebration organized on June 28 "to commemorate the American Stonewall homosexual movement anniversary" (He and Jolly 2002, 485). The abolishment of the crime of hooliganism, however, meant the risks associated with public discussions of homosexuality tangibly decreased, and this led to the creation of the first local NGOs and community groups (Cui 2009). One of the first informal organizations to be created was a pager hotline based in Beijing, the BP99575 hotline. He Xiaopei, one of the leading activists since the 1990s and a cofounder of the hotline, has written extensively about the beginning of the group:

> In the summer of 1997, six *tongzhi* living in Beijing (three foreign women, one Chinese man, one foreign man and myself) met together to discuss the potential and need for setting up a "*tongzhi* pager hotline." Some people suggested we should find a way to organize everyone. . . .
>
> By 1997 there already existed some *tongzhi* spaces, such as bars and discos, but many *tongzhi* did not know where to find them. . . . Having a space for *tongzhi* activities was very important to the *tongzhi* movement. Only if everyone comes out into the open can we move from "non-existence" or being a "phenomenon" to being visible living people. Only if everyone gets together can we move from being pitiable, solitary people, to being an organized political body with an agenda and struggle together for just treatment from society.

The hotline could provide information about the *tongzhi* scene, spaces and activities, and encourage more women and men to come out,[9] particularly women. Women *tongzhi* especially need to know where to find other women *tongzhi*. The hotline could become an early organizing, information and networking method. Compared with a telephone line, the beeper was more mobile, and even if discovered it would not be so easy to close down. (He and Jolly 2002, 481)

The creation of the hotline relied on a combination of local and foreign participants, and a distinct awareness of the need for a flexible style of organizing that could respond to a restrictive political environment. Although the grand goal of the hotline was to "organize everyone," its most important feature, according to He, was that of opening up possibilities for those tongzhi who were unaware of the existence of a community—especially women, who encountered the most barriers to participation. His words also reveal the hotline having an explicit, long-term political goal: by encouraging more and more tongzhi to participate in community gatherings, the hotline represented to its founders a possible path toward political advocacy. Much of the early, "first-wave" tongzhi organizing followed a similar logic: gatherings in bars and cafés, lala "salons" (discussion groups), hotlines, and informal meetings in private residences—all aimed at the creation of a visible community that could provide support and a sense of belonging to tongzhi all across the PRC—and that could perhaps, one day, fuel a more explicitly political tongzhi project.

The need for secrecy and flexibility He identifies should also be understood against the sociopolitical context of postsocialist China and, particularly, post-Tiananmen China. After 1989, governmental surveillance over public gatherings and political assembly has been a distinctive feature of the PRC, and one of the key legacies of 1989 is that independent groups in contemporary China are not allowed to engage in political activities or stage public events (Engebretsen 2014; Lei 2018). In the mid-1990s, the government implemented a registration system that would allow NGOs and civil society groups to operate legally as long as they registered as official organizations with the government. Although the registration requires groups to accept a certain governmental oversight, there are practical advantages to registering—such as official legal status and access to a variety of funding sources (Hildebrandt 2011). Tongzhi groups, however, are generally not allowed to register, and therefore, since the mid-1990s, they have had to contend with invisible boundaries setting the limits of what counts as a social vis-à-vis a political gathering.[10]

In addition to the risk of political repression, early tongzhi gatherings—and to a certain extent also later ones—had to contend with the dangers of social exposure. For tongzhi, one of the biggest risks is that of their identity as homosexuals being revealed to their family, classmates, or employers. This could potentially lead to serious consequences, including family rejection, removal from university programs, and dismissal from work. Therefore, the beginning of tongzhi organizing saw groups more focused on the establishment of a safe community and the creation of meeting places where tongzhi could meet without fear of being exposed to their heterosexual social circles. At the turn of the century, however, two dramatic changes accelerated the transition to a politicization of tongzhi groups and, in different ways, spurred the growth of the tongzhi community at an unprecedented rate: the HIV/AIDS epidemic and the diffusion of new information and communication technologies.

Becoming Political: Tongzhi Visibility during the AIDS Crisis

The AIDS outbreak at the end of the 1990s was one of the key factors spurring the emergence of tongzhi political activism and the single most significant source of funding for grassroots groups and organizations. The epidemic resulted in growing involvement from both the Chinese government—which increased AIDS-related funds from US$500,000 in 1996 to over US$10 million in 2001 (Hildebrandt 2012, 852)—and from transnational AIDS institutions, which were granted legitimacy for intervention in any country at the first UN General Assembly Special Session on HIV/AIDS in 2001. Tongzhi community leaders saw this as an opportunity to gain visibility in the public sphere, and to reduce the stigma connected to the pathologization of homosexuality as a mental illness (Long 2018). The public health crisis led to a recharacterization of tongzhi, who transitioned from being perceived as social deviants or mentally ill individuals to being a population at risk. This transition was made explicit in 2001, when the third edition of the *Chinese Classification of Mental Disorders* (*CCMD-3*) eliminated homosexuality from the list of mental diseases.

With homosexuality now officially decriminalized and depathologized, tongzhi stopped being a diagnostic category and emerged as social identity in the public sphere. Some tongzhi groups took the opportunity to become legally registered organizations by framing their work as a public health service (Engebretsen 2014), and for the first time, homosexuality started being discussed on government-controlled news outlets. On December 1, 2004, the Chinese Ministry of Health officially published statistics on male tongxinglian and rates of HIV infections among that population, and the information was made available on official state newspapers—including the *People's Daily* (*Renmin Ribao*), the official voice of the CCP. Two days after the article was published, China Central Television (CCTV) hosted the first televised discussion on homosexuality and AIDS, in a program titled 同性恋: 回避不如正视 *Tongxinglian: Huibi buru zhengshi* ("Homosexuality: Facing it rather than ignoring it"). The show opened with the following remarks:

> The Chinese government's Health Department released a new set of survey data the day before this year's "World's AIDS Day." . . .
>
> This is the first time that Chinese officials have released to the world figures on the number of male tongxinglian and HIV infection rates. What should we make of the fact that the previously hidden topic of homosexuality was officially discussed today, and what should we make of these numbers and the problem they represent? These are the key points we want to discuss today. The guests we invited today are the secretary general of the Chinese Society of Sexology, Professor Hu Peicheng of Peking University School of Medicine, and special commentator Xu Ge. A warm welcome to both of you. We should say that . . . today we are talking about homosexuality, and we should say that

it is still a relatively sensitive topic. We are discussing it here. We neither agree with nor criticize this behavior. More importantly, today we address it as an objective phenomenon.

The host tiptoed carefully around the topic of homosexuality, and his stated approach of neither agreeing nor criticizing the behavior is one of the first articulations of the official government position on tongzhi—one that still holds today. The position is known as the "three NOs policy" (三不政策 *san bu zhengce*), and it refers to the official governmental guidelines of "not encouraging, not discouraging, not promoting" homosexuality.[11] The position, while de facto being a nonpolicy, was still an improvement over earlier state-supported pathologization and resulted in tongzhi seeing their existence recognized for the first time on national television. In terms of representation, the kind of discourse promoted by the CCTV programming did result in a problematic and stigmatizing association of homosexuality and AIDS. At the same time, however, it also opened up opportunities for tongzhi groups to become visible players in the political arena—as long as they could frame their activities as responding to a government need (Hildebrandt 2012).

In addition to increased visibility, the state's involvement in responding to the AIDS epidemic also led to a notable increase in funding for grassroots NGOs. Transnational pressures further forced the central government to involve grassroots groups in official efforts—for example, in 2005 the Global Fund made participation of grassroots NGOs mandatory by making funding contingent on it (Long 2018). However, as the 2004 Ministry of Health report and the CCTV program exemplify, visibility and funding opportunities affected different parts of the tongzhi community in different ways. In particular, all instances of public discussion of homosexuality and AIDS focused exclusively on male tongzhi. This resulted in divergent trajectories of development for male and female tongzhi organizations, as the latter were often explicitly excluded from funding and prevention activities. Activists and community leaders active in those years often told me that unequal access to funding started introducing strains in the relationship between groups. While we were chatting over an oversized bowl of noodles in Beijing, Fan Popo, a prominent documentary filmmaker and activist, opened up about his frustration when organizing a traveling film festival in the early 2000s:

> So the funding for HIV/AIDS prevention . . . this money would only go to gay men, and not lesbians. So there was some tension between the two communities, also because the funding for a lot of events . . . they only accepted gay men. I remember when I was doing—I think this started in 2003, because that was the year when the Chinese government allowed more funding from abroad inside of China for HIV/AIDs prevention. . . . When we were putting together the Queer Film Festival tour, we tried to have a conversation with different groups in different cities, especially smaller cities rather than Beijing, Shanghai, Hangzhou. But a lot of the time they would say: "Sorry, we can only pay the travel fee of the gay men because this money is for the HIV/AIDS prevention." I was very pissed off.

Fan Popo here points to the damaging effect the situation had on the cohesion of the tongzhi community as a whole. By privileging male tongzhi groups, funding organization relegated female tongzhi to a subordinate, often invisible position. Simultaneous to the AIDS crisis creating new funding and networking opportunities for male tongzhi, a key technological development opened new possibilities for all grassroots groups in the PRC in the mid-2000s.

Online Activism

While the internet had reached the PRC in the 1990s, the number of users started growing exponentially in the new millennium, increasing from 620,000 registered users in 1997 to 87 million in 2004 and to over 253 million in 2008 (Statistical Survey on Internet Development in China).[12] The first tongzhi organization to explore the political possibilities of the new technology were women groups, in part because of the unavailability of any other venue for community formation. In my conversation with Xian,[13] the founder of Tongyu—the most influential lala organization in the PRC—and one of the founding members of the only transnational activist alliance linking the PRC, Taiwan, and

Hong Kong, she explained that in the absence of funding, the internet had strongly influenced the development of the lala community:

> [The invisibility of lesbians] of course, was related to HIV/AIDS funding and resources. And I would also say legitimacy, because . . . because of HIV/AIDS, the government had to kind of work with the gay men's community, but really they left lesbian women out all the time. They were still under the curtain, invisible, private. There was a lesbian bar at the time in Beijing. Like, one night. One night a week, and that was all. Basically, the websites were where the lesbian community was very active, people relied on the virtual space, because basically it's their whole lesbian life. Because in the real world, they still had to . . . well, be straight women.

Xian had come back to Beijing in 2004 after attending college and starting a PhD in the United States, from where she had also participated to transnational activist efforts under the guidance of Dr. Wan Yanhai, a prominent Chinese AIDS activist and human rights advocate. Upon her return in Beijing, she soon found that the female tongzhi community was mostly experiencing the invisibility that had characterized both male and female tongzhi groups before the AIDS crisis. She started leading a weekly salon in the outskirts of the capital, and then she turned to the web in order to attract other politically inclined participants.

> So [a friend] helped set up a website where we could announce the salon events. . . . In 2005, I . . . I thought the salon, I wished it to be a base for lesbians in Beijing, and from the salon I hoped to find people who were interested in activism so we could do more things. Later on, I published this post in a popular lesbian forum and I set up a group. Then we had the first offline meeting at what would later become a well-known lesbian bar, Xi Xian Fang, the West Wing. At the first meeting, we decided to call the group Tongyu, Common Language. That was in January 2005.

The name of the newly founded group was chosen in part due to the multiple layers of meaning embedded in it. Phonetically, the sound of *tongyu* (同语) is similar to 同女 *tongnü*, which is short for 女同性恋 *nü* (= female) *tongxinglian*, and it shares the first character, *tong*, with both *tongzhi* and *tongxinglian*. Furthermore, the English translation into "common language" was meant as a reference to the work of Adrienne Rich, whose first poetry collection published after she came out as lesbian in 1976 was titled *Dream of a Common Language*. Lastly, Xian explained to me that the idea of building a common language was a political statement on the part of the newly founded organization:

> Because the group, we didn't want it to be just a social group for lesbians. We wanted to do publications and advocacy. Again, at the time, lesbians were so invisible, so we wished to really create channels to the public, to talk about lesbian issues. That's kind of related to language, a common language. The idea is that although people can be of different sexualities or gender identities, we hope we can still understand each other in a way.

Similar to how the Beijing LGBT hotline functioned at the beginning of tongzhi activism, the internet became a way to raise awareness of tongzhi existence and, in many cases, a platform that could transform online community meetings into offline activism. The biggest change from pager-based organizing to web-based is, of course, one of scale: all of a sudden, grassroots groups found themselves armed with the possibility of reaching immense audiences with no geographical limits but those imposed by internet accessibility.[14] The beginning of online organizing opened up opportunities on an unprecedented scale, and tongzhi organizers today credit websites as the most important medium for information diffusion in contemporary China (Deklerck and Wei 2015). For tongzhi groups, the expansion of social media platforms at the end of the 2000s ultimately provided the most effective and relatively safe way for community building and organizing. In 2009, the creation of Sina Weibo (a micro-blogging platform similar to Twitter) coincided with the emergence of hundreds of new online tongzhi groups. Two years after that, the launch of WeChat in 2011 further shook the community, and WeChat-based tongzhi organizing is still the standard in 2021, at the time of this writing.

The transition to online organizing also led to an increased volume of transnational exchange, and from the standpoint of sexual identity had a profound impact especially on female tongzhi identity. In the early 2000s, coinciding with a rising tension between male and female groups, a new identity label started circulating among the female tongzhi community. Lesbians in the PRC started adopting the identity label 拉拉 *lala*, a term adapted from the Taiwanese slang term 拉子 *lazi*. The term comes from the nickname of the lesbian narrator in Qiu Miaojin's novel *Notes of a Crocodile*, a publication that has had a lasting impact on Taiwan's lesbian community.[15] While *tongzhi* is still considered a gender neutral term that encompasses everyone in the community, and it is used as such in contemporary tongzhi publications, it is not uncommon to hear the sentence "tongzhi and lala" used as a binary or to hear female-identified individuals using one label or the other depending on the occasion. For the younger generation of lala, the term has also become an empowering identity label that signifies political engagement, an abandonment of traditional patriarchal ideals, and a link to transnational conceptualizations of queer politics.

Between the explosion of online activism in the late-2000s and the time of my fieldwork in 2016–17, an unprecedented number of tongzhi groups have emerged all over the country, taking over the efforts of early informal organizations and gatherings. These groups, which form the landscape of contemporary tongzhi activism in the PRC, have had to contend with shrinking opportunities for civil society organizing in the switch from the Hu to the Xi administration (S. Zhao 2016). Amid tightening media control, crackdowns on free speech, and an increased governmental distrust for human rights activism (Cao and Hsu 2018; Lei 2018), tongzhi and lala communities continue to walk a tightrope between political visibility and exposure, continuously negotiating the discursive boundary between community engagement and identity politics.

"We Are Narrators": Queer Politics of Language

This chapter opened with a discussion of *queer* as a site of confusion, productive conversation, and potential tension. In this final section, I return to the term as an identity that has gained particular traction for a generation of young, urban, transnationally educated self-identified queer lala. The first issue of *Queer Lala Times* (*QLT*), an independent lala magazine, opened with the following statement (in English and Chinese), which was printed on all subsequent issues of the journal:

> We are *Lala*: we are not dissoluble under the umbrellas of "women," "gay," "homosexuality."
>
> We are queer; we are not content with the binarism of gay/straight, men/women, normal/pervert. We seek diverse narratives that speak to the complexity of the world, and we seek a more diverse reality.
>
> We are activists; with many others, we are committed to the gender/sexuality identity activism in China. The experience of changing convinces us that a change in mind is the ultimate pursuit in activism.
>
> We are narrators; we believe in the power of words.[16]

This opening statement directly connects queerness—understood as a fluidity that rejects binary understandings of sexuality—to being lala, and places it in opposition to other identity terms central to the community. In the Chinese version of the statement, *lala* is juxtaposed to *tongzhi* (translated as "gay") and *tongxinglian*, a provocation designed to question existing structures of power within the movement. The stance reflects a key strategy that lesbian groups resorted to when faced with the threat of invisibility and marginalization within the largest movement: the creation of "a coalition with bisexual and transgender people to fight against gay identity politics" (Bao 2018, 84). And yet, the final portion of the statement speaks to a search for a common goal and a shared ground to achieve it—leaving open possibilities for cooperation within and outside the national borders. Tellingly, despite the rejection of tongzhi in the opening statement the journal features multiple articles in which the term is used widely, sometimes as a gender neutral term, sometimes as a stand-in for "gay" and sometimes with the gendered qualifier *nü* to mean "female tongzhi."

The tension emerging from the deliberate juxtaposition of queer/lala and tongzhi in the *QLT* statement speaks to the historical legacy of the tongzhi movement in the PRC and to the politics of naming and labeling that have shaped the development of the community in the sinophone world. The contrast is similar to the linguistic bifurcation Leung (2008) identifies in Taiwan—where *ku'er* "approximates the theoretical and deconstructive stance of 'queer,' while [*tongzhi*] is associated with LGBT identity politics" (3). And yet the two terms juxtaposed refuse to fit neatly into a theoretical (abstract) versus identitarian (practical) dichotomy. The statement rejects a specific kind of identity politics focused on a homonormative tongzhi subject, but when paired with the recurrent use of the label in the journal articles it acts as a reminder of the radical power of fluid, ever-evolving language.

It is perhaps the concluding sentence of the *QLT* statement that best captures the work and political challenges of the contemporary tongzhi community. As the rest of this book explores, the political tongzhi project relies on narratives, on the creation and diffusion of discourses, and on the constant engagement with words and their impermanent meaning as a pathways toward change. In the chapters to come, I explore strategies for mobilization and political organizing, focusing particularly on the language of such strategies, on the discourses that inform them, and on the impact such linguistic and discursive choices have on their outcome.

2

Coming Out, Coming Home

Sexual Identity and Family Belonging

A few weeks before the 2015 Lunar New Year, a short movie titled 回家 *Hui Jia* (*Coming Home*) went viral on social media in the PRC. The video collected over 250 million views on qq.com, the website where it was originally posted, and was shared widely over micro-blogging and social media platforms such as Weibo and WeChat. The movie follows the story of Fang Chao, a young gay man and an exemplary "filial son" with top grades, a respectful disposition, and a successful career that allows him to shower his parents with gifts. Despite all this, he is strained by the pressure his family puts on him. Every year, his mother asks about his love life and hints at the need for grandchildren in the family. Crushed by the pressure and the weight of having to lie to his parents every year, Fang Chao decides to come out over the phone: "Mom, the thing is . . . I like guys." He is rejected by his parents, and for a full year, both sides suffer in silence and isolation. Then, while browsing the internet for information, Fang Chao's parents come across some articles on homosexuality and read a few stories from other families with gay children. Finally, on the eve of the following Lunar New Year's celebration, his mom picks up the phone and tearfully asks her son to come home. The film ends with a series of messages from mothers of young tongzhi: "Don't regard the love of your parents as a burden," says one. "Share the story of your life with your parents; they're willing to hear you out," suggests another. One of the last messages is addressed to parents: "Don't let traditional views of marriage get in the way of your child coming home."

To date, *Coming Home* is one of the most successful video campaigns organized by PFLAG, the largest tongzhi organization currently operating in the PRC. The timing of the release contributed to its success, as the Lunar New Year is a stressful time for Chinese youth. Most people studying or working away from home go back to visit their parents over the holidays, only to have their romantic lives thoroughly questioned and scrutinized. Pressure to find a partner is a burden shared by virtually all Chinese people in their twenties, as most parents want their child to get married and start a family. This expectation can be especially daunting for young tongzhi, as current Chinese law does not allow same-sex marriage, nor does it permit same-sex couples to adopt children. For tongzhi, coming out to their parents means exposing an impossibility to fulfill their role and duty as daughters and sons (Chou 2001; Rofel 2007). Many choose to stay away from home altogether or to enter marriages of convenience with partners of the opposite gender (*xinghun*) to avoid hurting their families (Choi and Luo 2016). Campaigns such as this short film aim to rewrite the meaning of coming out, presenting it as a process that ultimately strengthens the parent-child relationship.

In this chapter, I first introduce PFLAG as a tongzhi organization that considers family belonging as the central characteristic bringing members of the group—and Chinese tongzhi in general—together. I explore how belonging to a family system is emphasized as a shared identity within the group, and I analyze how PFLAG organizers strategically transform the meaning of tradition for this purpose. I then discuss the ways coming home narratives work to reinforce a sense of familial, social, and political belonging for young tongzhi, and I conclude reflecting on the implications of PFLAG's reliance on family and harmony discourses. On one side, I argue that the group's narrative and discursive choices serve the strategic purpose of displacing the political into the familial, opening up spaces for intervention and possibilities for change. On the other side, I also analyze the hidden costs of this strategy, as a narrative of harmonious belonging can also result in new erasures and exclusions.

Family, Harmony, and the Promise of Change

PFLAG was founded in Guangzhou in 2008 as an organization focused explicitly on tongzhi families—offering support and advice to tongzhi and their parents as they struggle to navigate family relationships. The Chinese name of the organization at the time of my fieldwork was 同性恋亲友会 Tongxinglian Qinyouhui (Homosexual Friends and Families Association), although most tongzhi referred to it as simply Qinyouhui or PFLAG in informal conversations. It has no formal ties with the U.S.-based PFLAG, although the English acronym does establish a connection through the family-oriented focus of both groups. In China, the cofounders are well-known figures among the tongzhi community: Wu Youjiang, also known as Wu Mama, was the first mother to publicly "come out" as supportive of her gay son in 2004 during a televised program on the topic of AIDS hosted on China's Guangzhou TV network; Ah Qiang, the current executive director, is an openly gay man and the public face of the group. During one of our conversations, Ah Qiang explained how his personal experience with his family informed his role as a cofounder:

> The reason why I decided to start this organization, a big reason has to do with my own experience. I myself am homosexual, and before she died, my mother would always ask me: "When will you get married, when will you bring a girlfriend home?" and for a long time, I told her, "Oh, you don't have to worry," or "I will explain later," you know, that is, I escaped, I evaded this. But then my mother died of her illness, and this made me feel like I had never told the truth to my own family. This made me feel really uncomfortable. I thought, there must be a lot of people in China like me. In fact, they may also face such a dilemma. Then I got the chance to start such an organization.

The chance, for Ah Qiang, was an in-person meeting with Wu Mama following a series of online exchanges on their respective blogs. Since the early days of the group, Ah Qiang envisioned as one of the principal goals for the organization the improvement of family relationships, and in particular the elimination of painful silences between parents and their children. With the help of a few core members, he started recruiting parents of tongzhi youth and encouraged them to share their stories—and their children's stories—with other parents. From an initial group of six families in Guangzhou, PFLAG has grown exponentially in its first ten years of operation and has now expanded to encompass almost all twenty-three provinces and all four municipalities in the PRC. At the time of this writing, the group counts over 100,000 members and eighty publicly active chapters, making it the largest and most visible tongzhi group in the country.

With its focus on young tongzhi and their families, PFLAG can be considered a sexual identity group—tongxinglian (homosexuality) is featured prominently in the organization's name, and PFLAG families are brought together by the presence of one or more family members who identify as tongzhi. However, the significant inclusion of parents as the main voice for the group points away from an understanding of tongzhi as an individual identity and presents, instead, the family as the focal point. Even the way most tongzhi refer to the organization emphasizes the family focus, as using Qinyouhui as shorthand removes homosexuality from the official name, effectively making PFLAG "the parents and friends association."

The organization emphasizes the predominance of family over individual identity in accordance with a cultural ideal that privileges the stability of family relationships above all. At the same time, the carefully constructed image of PFLAG also suggests a strategic motive behind this family-centered framing. This strategy is evident in the organization's stated goals, which PFLAG's official website presents as follows: "To enhance understanding and communication between homosexuals and their relatives and friends, and to create a harmonious living environment for homosexuals [和谐的同性恋生活环境]." On one side, the mention of harmony (和谐 *hexie*) explicitly ties the group's objective to a Confucian ideal of social harmony. This reference to Confucian ethics decenters individual sexual identity in favor of a cultural identity that establishes belonging through a shared desire to maintain a harmonious relation with family of origin, as much as through a shared sexual identity. On the other side, the reference to harmony also signals *political* belonging: in 2008, when PFLAG was founded, "harmonious society" (*hexie shehui*) was the signature slogan of Hu Jintao's presidency and the leading policy discourse in the PRC (Guo and Guo 2008). The notion of a "harmonious living environment" (*hexie huanjin*) closely mirrors President Hu's favored phrase.

Both as a reference to tradition and as a signal of political belonging, harmony constitutes a potential source of tension for PFLAG. The group defines its core mission as one that fundamentally promotes change: "To help more people to accept homosexual friends and relatives around them and encourage them to take a stand (站出来 *zhanchulai*) to improve the visibility and the living space of the homosexual community." This creates a paradox: How can the group fulfill its objective of promoting harmony, while simultaneously advocating for its members to stand up and demand visibility? Subscribing to a state-enforced harmony discourse makes change difficult, because questioning existing social norms disrupts harmony.

The verb 站出来 *zhanchulai* in PFLAG's core mission statement perfectly encapsulates this dilemma: the term is a combination of *zhan*, "standing up"; *chu*, "moving outward" (but also a reference to 出柜 *chu gui*, "coming out of the closet"); and *lai*, "to come (toward the speaker)." In a sense, the verb is simultaneously communicating the idea of taking a stand, of coming out, and of moving toward a community of compassionate parents and children. PFLAG's work builds precisely on the dynamic tension emerging when these seemingly contradictory notions are brought together. To achieve this, organizers and participants act on multiple fronts: they discursively deconstruct specific notions of tradition while promoting others; they rely on public performances of coming home narratives; and they strategically employ harmony to move toward a conceptualization of change as nondisruptive and nonoppositional.

The Discursive Legacy of Coming Home

PFLAG's terminology on coming out as "coming home" is a familiar one to scholars studying nonnormative sexual identities in the sinophone world. Hong Kong scholar and activist Chou Wah-Shan (2000, 2001) was the first to apply the term to tongzhi, using it to describe a culturally specific strategy queer subjects were using to navigate the social arena of the family. His argument, which has had a lasting impact on the tongzhi community, was crafted in response to the diffusion of the Western hegemonic discourse on coming out: resisting homogenizing interpretations that risked erasing cultural specificity, Chou argued instead that in Chinese societies families are more likely to accept a child's homosexual orientation if the topic is never explicitly breached but rather implicitly suggested. According to Chou, tongzhi can successfully "come home" by introducing their partner to their family without acknowledging the existence of a sexual or amorous relationship between them (ibid.).

While Chou's work has been recognized as a key contribution to a postcolonial and decolonial project of resisting Western hegemonic narratives (Bao 2018; Huang and Brouwer 2018; Kam 2013), it has also been met with controversy and has been critiqued for its cultural essentialism and for its interpretation of nonphysical repression of deviance as "a kind of cultural tolerance towards homosexuality in China" (Kam 2013, 92). Chou relies on a dichotomous opposition of a Western coming out (vocal, aggressive, disruptive) and a Chinese coming home (silent, submissive, harmonious). In his conceptualization, tongzhi avoid disharmony by silencing themselves, erasing their narratives and visible existence. In an influential critique of Chou's coming home argument, Taiwan scholars Liu Jen-peng and Ding Naifei (2005) call this strategy a form of "reticent poetics" and identify it as a form of homophobic violence that operates by forcing queer subjects into silent invisibility.

Despite the controversy, Chou's conceptualization of a "coming out vs. coming home" dichotomy still resonates strongly with members of the tongzhi community. Over the course of multiple conversations and interviews with tongzhi, I saw the juxtaposition between a pursuit of individual desires and the fulfillment of family hopes emerge as an explanation of tongzhi resistance to coming out to their parents. More than once, participants conceptualized this tension using a framework similar to Chou's, presenting it as "Western vs. Chinese way of thinking." This happened, for example, during my interview with Wind, a volunteer in PFLAG's Shanghai chapter. We had initially connected online during my first trip to China, and he was the tongzhi who had clued me to some of the larger events that had at that time been in the works to celebrate the ten years of PFLAG's activities. At forty years of age, he was one of the older tongzhi in the group, which he discovered after moving to Shanghai from a smaller city in northwestern China. Before becoming acquainted with PFLAG, he had entered into a xing-hun, marrying a lesbian friend with the hope of appeasing his parents. He explained his choice, drawing on a West-China dichotomy:

> China has this type of culture, "I would rather sacrifice myself in order to make my parents happy." However, Americans are different. Americans and Westerners think, "I want to be happy. Perhaps if I'm happy, then others will be happy." A different way of thinking results in different choices. Most people here think, "I would rather marry a girl, or do this or that . . . I would rather hide myself if it means my parents are happy."

From Wind's perspective, coming out to his parents would have been a selfish choice made in pursuit of individual happiness. Staying in the closet and marrying a woman was the only way to fulfill his duty as a son. Sexual identity here is squarely placed in the context of a kinship system, and understood almost solely for its effect to potentially disrupt it. Despite recognizing potential benefits such as individual happiness, Wind felt what he would gain personally would be eclipsed by the harm that would come to his parents.

After a few years of xinghun, however, Wind and his boyfriend started questioning their decision. After reading numerous online articles and hearing the stories of tongzhi who had revealed themselves to their families, Wind realized that being in a xinghun forced him and his partner in a situation where they constantly had to lie to their parents. In 2014, they both decided to come out to their respective families. Wind's parents stopped talking to him for a few months, but he slowly convinced them to read a few PFLAG articles online and finally persuaded them to participate in one of their meetings. It took almost a full year, but as he explained, "the process couldn't be rushed." At the time of our talk in 2017, he had rebuilt a strong connection with both his parents and the three of them were regular attendees and volunteers at PFLAG events. Wind and his partner shared an apartment with his partner's mother, and they both worked in a small family company founded together with Wind's father. Although he could well understand why tongzhi would stay in the closet in order to protect their parents, his experience of coming out and his participation in PFLAG's activities had changed his mind about the key to parents' happiness:

> Those parents who have been relieved [of the burden of a traditional family model], compared to other Chinese parents, I think they are the happiest people. . . . It may be because they need to learn to accept their child, and this leads to even bigger changes. It leads to lifestyle changes, to an opening of one's inner world and a change of mindset. That's why PFLAG is so great.

Wind's story exposes the tension on which PFLAG's harmony discourse is predicated: if a traditional understanding of Confucian harmony supports the idea that children should respect their parents, the crux of the matter becomes whether lying for their sake is more respectful than causing some pain in order to attain a more honest relationship. PFLAG's rhetoric strongly emphasizes the latter as the only choice that can lead to a strong parent-child relationship. As such, the organization's leaders are vocal advocates of coming out. This position requires them to undermine Chou's understanding of coming out as a Western import in opposition to a "Chinese choice" of staying in the closet. The group achieves that by questioning the common conceptualization of coming out and coming home as antithetical (D. Wong 2007)—that is, questioning the dichotomous understanding of coming out as signaling a move away from the family and toward sexual freedom and coming home as a move toward the family and as a suppression of queer desires (Huang and Brouwer 2018). Challenging an understanding of coming home as an erasure of queer subjectivities, PFLAG suggests the opposite: coming home necessarily involves an explicit acknowledgment of tongzhi existence as a way to reclaim tongzhi cultural belonging in the family-kinship system.

Rethinking Coming Home: Questioning Static Notions of Tradition

Wind's narrative, particularly as it concerns his change of heart on the decision to come out to his parents, is a fitting example to unpack the discursive shift that allows PFLAG to align coming home to tongzhi visibility rather than erasure. The shift happens through a key reframing of the notion of "tradition." Before his exposure to PFLAG, Wind justified his decision to stay in the closet through a view of Chinese culture as one of silent sacrifice, where parents' happiness depends on their children respecting the rules of tradition. While parental happiness remains a priority in the second quote, it becomes dependent on *change*—and, to a great extent, on an *abandonment* of traditional models. Tradition is thus transformed: it no longer is the key to family happiness but rather it is an obstacle to it. The reframing allows for the simultaneous reinforcing of culturally powerful traditional concepts (such as filial piety and respect for one's parents), and the undermining of notions of tradition that are antithetical to change (such as compulsory heterosexual marriage).

Following this logic, many PFLAG volunteers adopt the language of tradition to talk about what they see as an obstacle to positive social development. Traditional understandings of family are depicted as a burden afflicting the older generations, and PFLAG's work is metaphorically presented as a medicine that can ease the parents' pain and help them live a happier life. Oak, a twenty-six-year-old tongzhi I met at a PFLAG event, saw his parents' change in attitude in a similar way as Wind. Oak had been out for three years when we met, and he described his coming out as an ongoing process:

> The concept of traditional family is deeply rooted; for example, my parents say I need to get married, have a baby, and things like that. Because this concept is like a seed. If it's planted in your heart, it's really difficult to change, although it can change, but it's more difficult for them.

By linking traditional understandings of family to a deeply rooted plant, Oak's account simultaneously points to how difficult it is to change them, and acknowledges the possibility for change. For Oak, the important part was not pressuring his father into immediate acceptance but rather slowly exposing him to new possibilities through gradual contact with other PFLAG parents, events, and articles.

I gave my father three years; I think time really is like a medicine. And now my father is much calmer, more serene in his heart; it's not like in the beginning when there was a lot of opposition and things of that sort. Family really is the most important thing.

As in Wind's case, the successful outcome is achieved by simultaneously reframing traditional ideas about family as an obstacle to positive change, while emphasizing continuity with tradition through the idea of harmony. Oak's father's improved mental health and mood is presented as a movement toward harmony and away from tradition. The apparent paradox can be explained as a juxtaposition of two kinds of tradition: one is static and damaging in its opposition to change; the other is dynamic and can promote and anchor change.

The labeling of unchanging traditional ideas about family and marriage as potentially disruptive was common among PFLAG parents as well. Oftentimes, in fact, parents were particularly critical of behaviors that they saw as misguidedly attached to tradition. During a lunch in Shanghai with two veteran PFLAG moms, both of whom had been involved with the group for over four years, the conversation veered toward the phenomenon of tongqi, a term used to describe the unaware wives of tongzhi men, which led to the following exchange:

> WOOL MAMA: That's how selfish people think. He [a tongzhi acquaintance who married a girl without telling her he is gay] is really selfish.
> SALT MAMA: He is married and even has a child. He told me that the most important thing in life is to marry and have a child.
> WOOL MAMA [*shaking her head*]: Such a traditional mindset. So selfish.

The exchange turns the idea of traditional selfless behavior, which Wind used to justify the choice of not coming out for the sake of his parents, on its head: hiding one's sexuality for the sake of tradition is no longer presented as the filial, dutiful course of action but rather as a type of selfish and inconsiderate behavior. Wool Mama and Salt Mama judge the idea of lying to one's spouse and family in order to blindly follow "tradition" selfish. Tradition becomes an obstacle to others' happiness as well as to one's personal development and appears to be used in opposition to a modern, changed, more open mindset.

In a similar twist, behaviors traditionally considered selfish were often transformed into positive outcomes of a process of development triggered in parents by their sons and daughters coming out. At the same lunch conversation, Salt Mama reflected on the practical benefits of her son not having children:

> Having a child is such a pain. They are a lot of work and then they get sick, and they have problems with their teeth, and it's just tiring. In China, when one becomes a grandma, then one has to help take care of the baby. And that is so tiring! I see those mothers who have become grandmothers, and their skin is so gray and they are always tired and they can never relax. Why are we raised thinking that this is the right thing to do? It's much better if we're not grandmas! We can travel and relax, and we can enjoy our time.

Her sentiment was shared by many other PFLAG parents I talked to, most of whom expressed happiness and relief at the thought of being liberated by the burden of grandparenthood. Many saw it as an opportunity for personal growth and as a way to create new personal connections with other tongzhi parents as well as with their own sons and daughters.

On more than one occasion, I heard parents describe their child's coming out as the opening of a new door, as an opportunity for a future they had never before considered. For example, on an early morning in June, I found myself chatting with Sage Mama while looking at the sunrise over the East China Sea. I had met her son, Birch, a few days prior when he had told me his story. He had come out to her a first time while he was studying for his college examination, but she had brushed it off and attributed his words to stress. At the same time, she gave him some encouraging signals, by telling him "if one day you find out you really are [gay], tell me." Years later, he came out to her again after meeting his boyfriend, and she agreed to attend a PFLAG event with him. That June morning, Sage Mama was on the upper deck of our ship doing her morning exercises, and as I joined her, I made a comment about the beautiful sunrise. She smiled and looked at the sun:

> You know, I used to see this every day when I was little. And not because I wanted to see the pretty sunrise, but because I had to work in the field. You know what I thought? At the time, I thought the sun was coming out from the dirt, this big ball of fire emerging from nowhere. And now look at me! I never would have thought I would experience all this [referring to PFLAG events that we had attended in the previous days]. I thought I would just become a grandmother. This is what we do here [in China], if you look at what parents do, everyone has children and then takes care of children and grandchildren. They stay in our house, and we care for the baby. I had never thought to question that. My son is gay, so he probably won't have children. [She turns and smiles at me] So I don't have to worry about that!

Just like Salt Mama, Sage Mama framed the lack of grandchildren not as a loss but as an opportunity for growth and discovery. The sunrise parallel is telling: just like she had never questioned the sun coming up from the earth when she was little, she had also never dared to question social expectations and her future as a grandmother. But her son's coming out had freed her from the traditional social role she thought she was destined for.

This reframing of unchanging traditional behavior as an obstacle to growth is what allows PFLAG to untangle the project of coming out away from a dichotomized China-West opposition, making it instead a central force for social change. In this light, coming out has practical social implications because, aside from promoting positive visibility, it strengthens a cross-generational alliance and opens up possibilities for change within deeply rooted cultural traditions. Confucian principles such as harmony and respect for one's parents are never questioned, nor are they negatively assigned a "traditional" label, as they are unshackled from a static understanding of what being a filial son or daughter means.

Yet coming out to one's parents, while necessary, is an insufficient condition for tongzhi social belonging. Coming out makes the tongzhi identity visible in the family and results in strengthened ties between parents and children, but it is acceptance through the process of coming *home* that, in PFLAG's discourse, transform family belonging into social belonging. The transformation plays on a metonymical understanding of family as the site of social belonging, and reflects "discursive productions of family [as] indispensable sites for establishing one's humanness as well as one's social subjectivity" (Rofel 1999, 463). In other words, if social belonging is predicated on the maintenance of social harmony, a strengthening of family ties based on parental acceptance proves that tongzhi pose no threat to social stability. Family acceptance acts as a protective force, shielding tongzhi from the risk of being perceived as a community of outsiders in society.

As a way to promote a narrative of belonging, PFLAG organizers put particular emphasis on the importance of sharing successful coming home stories. In the early days of the group, before the organization had an official website or a WeChat account, one of the first activities founders put together to draw the attention of potential members was a long blog post collecting the stories of a few parents who had accepted the fact that their child was a tongzhi. The online traffic increased exposure for the in-person meetings that have always been a signature event for PFLAG: their public parents-children sharing sessions.

Coming Home Narratives

Since its founding in 2008, PFLAG has organized an annual *kentanhui* ("forum," sometimes translated as "conference") every summer. The event started as a small meeting of six families in Guangzhou the first year and progressively grew into an elaborate multiday event involving hundreds of participants. The evolution of the kentanhui throughout the years displays a shift from despair to happiness that mirrors the change in the meaning of "traditional": old-timers who had participated in the early meetings were all in agreement as they explained to me how these events used to be characterized by a lot of crying, while now they look more like a party and a celebration of family ties.

The 2017 meeting was indeed a celebration of sorts, as it marked the tenth anniversary of the first meeting. To honor the occasion, the annual June kentanhui took place on a cruise ship traveling from Shanghai to Fukuoka, Japan. The ambitious project was planned over the course of a year, and it gathered roughly eight hundred participants. The 2017 program included reflections on ten years of PFLAG activity, panels on effective strategies to come out without upsetting one's parents, updates from regional chapters, a panel on U.S.-based surrogacy programs, and—for the first time in the history of the PRC—a collective same-sex wedding ceremony. As with previous kentanhui, however, the central feature of the 2017 meeting remained the parent-child sharing session.

PFLAG's sharing sessions take the form of a public conversation where parents talk about their experience with their children's coming out. These conversation events typically happen on a stage, with two or three speakers in chairs facing the public. A parent, guided by the questions of a moderator, recounts the experience of their child coming out, and sometimes, the child in question participates in the discussion. While each parent has a unique story to tell, the structure of these narratives is often strikingly similar to that depicted in PFLAG's *Coming Home* campaign film. As an opener to the 2017 sharing session, the movie was projected on a large screen in the ship's auditorium, and it was enthusiastically received by the crowd.

After the movie ended, heavy curtains covered the screen and the focal center of attention became the three chairs to the left of the stage. One of the first coming home stories was that of Wolf Mama, a group veteran from Suzhou who had participated in previous sharing sessions. She explained her daughter first started dropping a few hints during middle school: "[My daughter] said 'Mom, I might not get married in the future.' I asked why, and she said 'Mom, I don't want to hurt others, I don't want to hurt others.' I asked why, and she said 'No reason, I don't want to get married.'" The exchange reproduces a fairly typical approach to coming out, one that previous scholars have identified as an indirect way of "not laying it bare"—a strategy that relies on avoiding identity labels while privileging subtle hints that indicate same-sex desire (Bie and Tang 2016; S. Huang 2016, 105–6). Expressing one's desire for not hurting others is one of the methods my participants most commonly used to broach the subject with their family. While refusal to marry is interpreted as a potentially shameful choice and can be seen as disrespectful toward the parents, such refusal is paired with an explanation that highlights the moral character of the child. This pairing sets the stage for a ground-shifting realization: ignoring (or pretending to ignore) the existence of same-sex desire will ultimately result in negative social consequences while acknowledging it and understanding it will lead to stability. In the case of Wolf Mama's daughter, her indirect approach didn't produce the desired effect, so she tried a different strategy:

> She never actually told me, she didn't dare—she told me afterward she didn't dare to say that word in front of me, those three characters, *tong xing lian*. To tell you the truth, she used a very silly approach. One day, I don't exactly remember when, it must have been 2012 or 2013, . . . she sneakily added me to the PFLAG parents chat on QQ. . . . So one day I found out I had this group chat on my phone, and I was very curious, so I opened it and after a short while, many parents greeted me, hello, hello, Mom this and Mom that, and they said our children are gay but it doesn't matter, our children are gay.

While much more explicit in her second coming out, Wolf Mama's daughter kept avoiding direct confrontation and the explicit use of identity labels. Adding her mom to the PFLAG parents' chat also achieved dual goals for her: on one side, it amounted to declaring that she was tongxinglian (homosexual), and on the other side, the lively conversation on the parents' chat indirectly normalized her sexuality by giving it a place within society and, more specifically, within the family. In other words, if so many other parents and families were going through this and still supporting their tongzhi son or daughter, could it really be so unacceptable?

After realizing the meaning of her daughter's early hints, Wolf Mama experienced a difficult period characterized by little contact with her daughter, lack of sleep, and a pain that she described as "the uncomfortable feeling of a needle stuck in my heart." After a few heated conversations on the QQ group with other parents, she muted the discussion. Three months later, however, she felt compelled to go back to the group chat:

So I opened this [parents' support] group again, and after I opened it, I did not write anything. I quietly watched the parents chatting inside and then checked out the links they shared, the videos, the articles. I eagerly opened every link and every article, and I felt much better after reading, because before I was thinking, how can it be that my own child is gay, because I had never encountered anyone who was gay, the concept of gay didn't exist for me. Then one day I saw in the group that there was a meeting in Wuxi, my daughter knew about that, so I told her, we should go see the sharing session.

The resolution mirrors almost exactly the one presented in *Coming Home*, as the parent-child reconciliation takes place after Wolf Mama learns new information and becomes acquainted with a world that was completely foreign to her before her interaction with other PFLAG parents.

Even though both sides of the interaction experience pain through the process of coming home, stories such as this avoid assigning blame or painting the parents' reaction in a negative light. Rather, cultural traditions and "traditional ideas" (*chuantong xiangfa*) are often held accountable for the initial misunderstanding. Wolf Mama concluded her story with a call to other parents to learn from her experience:

I want to tell other parents that if you love your children, you must accept everything about your child! As long as our children live happily and healthily, maintaining face is of secondary importance, you are the source of your own fear. Now I've also come out with other relatives, and our relationship is harmonious, we all care about and love my daughter. Children, be brave! The sun shines so much brighter outside the closet!

Wolf Mama's conclusion reinforces some of the notions discussed earlier: far from being an individual experience, coming out becomes a family endeavor, to the point that by the end of the story the parents themselves are the ones coming out. The explicit reference to harmony drives the point further home, as it emphasizes the strengthening of family ties as a positive outcome of the difficult process. Furthermore, while certain cultural traditions—such as love for one's child—are upheld as vital guiding principles in the parent-child relationship, other traditions, such as the need to maintain face, are exposed as obstacles that get in the way of harmonious family dynamics.

Stories like this one are fairly standard for sharing sessions, and kentanhui veterans like Wolf Mama tend to rely on the language of the organization more often than "new parents." Stories from first-time attendees, however, carry other important benefits: new faces underline how much the group is growing, and stories told for the first time are often emotionally charged and generate a powerful response in the public. This became evident on the cruise when Marble Mama took the stage to share her daughter's story for the first time. Marble Mama had discovered PFLAG only a few months prior, in April 2017, and had attended a sharing session in Wuhan. The cruise sharing session was her first time speaking in front of an audience and her first time telling her story to anyone in standard Mandarin rather than dialect. Her daughter, Crane, sat next to her during the sharing session, helping her through the narration. Crane had initially come out to her when she was in high school, but the first time, her mother had completely ignored her and dismissed her ideas about liking women as youthful confusion. A few years after that first conversation and following a breakup with her girlfriend, Crane tried again:

> I talked to my mother, and I said, "I like girls," and then I gave her this video to watch, to see what she would say, but she wouldn't watch. She didn't want to watch. She ignored me. My mother spoke very calmly, she said only one sentence; I heard it very clearly. She said: "Out of all the people in all the surrounding villages, you are the only pervert." Because my mother didn't know there were actually many [tongzhi] around us. I had seen many people from nearby villages on apps such as Blued, LesDo,[1] so, so many. But I didn't tell my mother.

Just like Wolf Mama's son, Crane came out "indirectly," trying to have other parents speak for her through a PFLAG video and emphasizing behavior over sexual identity. During a later conversation we had on the ship, she explained to me that she didn't want to alienate her mother with terms she couldn't possibly know. After Crane's second coming out, Marble Mama avoided her daughter for months. Crane tried to convince her to talk by telling her that she felt alone "with a brick on [her] heart," but her mom was determined to ignore her. In the end, Crane tricked her mom to go to the city with her under the pretense of buying some new clothes and brought her to a PFLAG meeting instead. Marble Mama still judged the move too bold and playfully scolded her daughter during the sharing session. But she acknowledged that talking to other parents had helped her.

> She was trying to get rid of that brick in her heart, and I didn't talk to her for half a month, with no interruption. When she got home after work, I went to sleep. When she went to work in the morning, I slept. I didn't bother to care for her. Later, I realized my good home was not good at all. I wanted to provide my precious daughter with a good home. By making her happy, I achieved my own happiness.

As the narrative reached the moment of resolution, Marble Mama started to cry and to apologize to her daughter for not understanding her at first. Switching back and forth between standard Mandarin and dialect, she recalled growing up in poverty and having to take care of her daughter alone after the death of her husband. Everyone in the audience encouraged mother and daughter to hug, and by the end of the session, there were teary eyes all around.

Whether told by veteran volunteers or first-time attendees, coming home stories such as the two analyzed here tend to rely on a structured narration that identifies three pivotal moments in the coming out process: a first moment of misunderstanding, a phase in which change begins to happen, and a final reconciliation. The initial misunderstanding is often presented as being caused by lack of information or by incorrect interpretation and associated with static traditional understandings of sexuality and family duty. This usually leads to parents rejecting their child and causes family fragmentation, which makes this phase the most challenging and painful one for both parties. The transformative phase is usually triggered through parents' exposure to conversations that they previously ignored or that they had never heard. Understanding is the result of this newly acquired knowledge. The final reconciliation stabilizes relationships within the family but also solidifies the newly established connection with other parents of tong-zhi. This phase signals harmony both within and outside the family as the positive outcome of the process.

This narrative structure assumes multiple levels of significance in the context of the tongzhi movement. The three phases are articulated following the complicated emotional response of parents and are meant to elicit an equally strong emotional reaction in the audience—even the minimal setup of the sharing session is meant to literally put emotions center stage. From a social movement perspective, if we consider emotions as "involv[ing] beliefs and assumptions open to cognitive persuasion" (Jasper 1998, 401), this becomes key to the creation of a narrative where change is possible. The initial negative response is presented as tied to an incomplete knowledge, which leads to a reading of the child's sexuality as an infraction of moral/cultural values. Once the knowledge void is filled, however, reconciliation becomes possible, and the conversation fulfills an important therapeutic effect.

The resolution of the narrative in a reunification also speaks to the community- and identity-building function that coming home stories aim to fulfill. Stories most often conclude with speakers hugging each other, and the public partakes in the experience with tears, loud words of encouragement, and applause. Scholars have shown that stories shared by movement participants can serve to create or reinforce a collective identity (Polletta 2006; Polletta and Jasper 2001), and in this case, the public nature of the experience does allow tongzhi families in the audience to see their own experience reflected in that of the speakers. After attending a sharing session, many audience members choose to become speakers in future sessions and forge strong personal ties with the families that played a role in their decision to become active members of the PFLAG community. Importantly, although the sexual identity of their children is the central element that brings most of those families together, sharing sessions establish that their common characteristic is the fact that they all value the strength of family ties, and have decided to change in order to achieve a balanced and harmonious parent-child relationship.

The narrative structure of coming home stories becomes politically significant when one considers that historically the Chinese family has been understood as a microcosm of society writ-large and that the parent-child relationship is a small-scale representation of the state-citizen relationship (Tamura et al. 1997). As the parental figure becomes symbolic of the Chinese government, the child comes to represent the tongzhi community at large. Coming out and becoming visible is done with no intent to create friction but rather as a way to ask for inclusion and to establish a deeper connection with a beloved authority figure. Even if the parents' emotional response appears as the cause of the initial suffering, such reaction is never labeled as inappropriate and there is no blame assigned on either side. The rejection is presented as being in line with current, albeit outdated, cultural and social standards, which make an initial misunderstanding almost inevitable. The second phase in the narration, in which change begins to happen, therefore presents PFLAG—as an organization and a community—as the key to fix the broken relationship, and as the source of new knowledge that can avoid any more suffering. The final reconciliation symbolically represents the goal of the tongzhi community as articulated in PFLAG: understanding, positive visibility, and inclusion in the family-society in which tongzhi belong.

The analogy in coming home stories points to tongzhi groups and community as the potential educators of a well-meaning but underinformed authority while also suggesting that a direct and confrontational method of self-assertion is likely to cause more friction than to be a source of significant change. As I show in the following section, the language of harmony is a strategically useful political alternative to contention.

Strategic Harmony

On one side, PFLAG's focus on family, and particularly on the child-parent relationship, is a direct consequence of the social environment in which tongzhi groups are operating: in absence of governmental and religious oppression, the family is the social space where tongzhi encounter the most pressure. And since family is one of the main sites of struggle for members of the community (Brainer 2018, 2019; Engebretsen 2009; Kam 2013; Rofel 2007; D. Wong 2007), PFLAG's goals can be understood as a response to this pressure. Their mobilization of a harmony-related discourse is a way to appeal to a shared cultural understanding of filial behavior while simultaneously signaling that tradition and change can coexist. On the other side, as pointed out earlier, appealing to harmony is also a strategic choice that signals political belonging by mirroring state-enforced discourses on social harmony.

The rhetorical and cultural power of a harmony-centered discourse is not lost on PFLAG organizers, and seasoned speakers rely on it often during events and sharing sessions. In some cases, when speakers do not explicitly rely on the concept of harmony, their words are still filtered through that frame in official reports published by the organization. This happened during the 2017 sharing session with the story of Fern Mama, who, after joining PFLAG, used the group to find a boyfriend for her son. During the cruise sharing session, the conversation concerning her son's coming out went as follows:

> FERN MAMA: My son came out early, he came out ten years ago.
> MODERATOR: And you accepted him at the time, right?
> FERN MAMA: It's because he talked to me often. Also, I love him very much. He is a very honest boy, and I really trust him. [The coming out process] is painful for every parent, but my pain was short-lived.

In the WeChat article published on the official PFLAG account, however, her words were rendered as: "My son came out 10 years ago. Because of our very good parent-child relationship and harmonious communication, I experienced almost no pain and I accepted my child relatively smoothly." While the content of the exchange hasn't been altered in any dramatic way, the written report emphasizes harmony much more strongly than the original conversation. In addition to that, the article as a whole introduced the sharing session with the subheading "Breaking and rebuilding, building an equal and harmonious parent-child relationship." The reason for such a strong emphasis on harmony is political as much as cultural. After a few conversations with PFLAG volunteers, I realized the concept of harmony was often used in contrast to rights and rights-based organizing. For example, during an interview with Feather, a PFLAG volunteer and one of the main organizers of activities in Hangzhou, he discussed where he saw the limits of rights-based organizing in China's political environment:

> After all, since we are a one-party country and are under the leadership of the Communist Party, we cannot do too many things in terms of our rights and interests. Because, as you can understand, because of the government, our historical tradition is like this, we care and pay attention to the Doctrine of the Mean.

The Doctrine of the Mean is a direct reference to Confucius, and it once again encapsulates the idea that each person should strive for balance and harmony. Following the path of the mean requires individuals to act in accordance to the natural balance of things, elevating moderation, sincerity, and propriety as key qualities to cultivate. In the context of the tongzhi movement, following the path of the mean is also a key strategic choice. PFLAG organizers recognize the coercive power of a state-enforced harmony and model their rhetoric to avoid breaking certain unwritten rules of political engagement. For example, Feather once explained to me how China's political situation informs the identity of PFLAG volunteers, saying: "In fact, our group of volunteers cannot use the word *activist*; we are more like participants. Because you see, in China—China is a very harmonious country [lit. "a golden mean country"]. The government very much hopes we can be gentle and cooperative." The mention of the golden mean, and thus the reference to Confucian social harmony, demonstrates once again a full awareness on the part of PFLAG volunteers of the thin line separating harmonious and contentious behavior.

Placing such strong emphasis on state-approved harmony rhetoric may seem to speak to a weakening or even an abandonment of the political and social tongzhi project—after all, Feather's words about not being able to use the label "activist" suggest a certain level of self-censorship and policing within the group. However, alignment with state discourses is a critical step that allows PFLAG to have a public presence as an organization. The avoidance of explicitly political labels in favor of organizational identities that can be more easily read as "public service" is a common strategy for grassroots groups and organizations in the PRC (Engebretsen 2014; Hildebrandt 2013; Wu 2017). For PFLAG, achieving the middle ground means operating in a position of constant tension between stability and change, harmony and visibility. Opportunities for change emerge from this dynamic tension, as tongzhi are invited to zhanchulai—to stand up, to come out, to come home. The key term that opened this chapter came up often in conversation with PFLAG members, contextualized as a pathway to change. Oak, for example, addressed it as a key strategy for the younger generation of tongzhi:

> It is not like before. I heard a lot of stories from the older generation; they had to go to secret strategic places, and there were places where you couldn't be like that. So I think in these years, actually I think social acceptance will grow larger and larger. I mean, this is how the process works and what needs to happen, it's possible that when you first come out, people won't accept you, but we all need this process, if you don't take a stand [站 出来 zhanchulai], it could be that twenty years go by and nothing has changed.

For Oak, as for many other tongzhi in PFLAG, reclaiming belonging within the family is part of a process of standing up and reclaiming belonging in society. The political implications of standing up together as a community are clear and potentially risky, especially since the Chinese state routinely adopts a "divide and rule" approach to minimize the chances of social groups joining together (Lei 2018; Perry 2007). In this case, however, the political implications of tongzhi youth teaming up with their relatives are eclipsed by the fact that a positive parent-child relationship is at the basis of social stability. Pushing for an alliance of this kind effectively displaces the political (standing up for tongzhi visibility) into the familial (standing up for one's child), allowing PFLAG to minimize their contentiousness while emphasizing their work as a social service organization in favor of harmony.

So how does this displacement contribute to a project of change? When voicing their vision for social change, PFLAG members articulated an approach that they qualified as "bottom-up" but that presents significant differences from the grassroots model of contention that the label evokes. Bear Baba, one of the first fathers to join PFLAG and one of the most active in the arena of video and documentary production, explained what he meant with "bottom-up change" as follows:

> There have been so many changes . . . from the perspective of a single person, so many people had no idea what homosexuality was. Now they do. But we need to keep talking about it: if we don't talk about it, how will they know what homosexuality is? I didn't know! When my son came out, I had no idea. From the perspective of the group, a great deal of things have changed. Before it was only a few people, they were all crying. Now there are so many and they are so happy. From the perspective of society, there is more understanding now. China is like that: it's hard to change things from the top down [i.e., influencing the government]; it's easier to start from the bottom. China works like that. If enough people are talking and discussing an issue, then people in power will pay attention. If there are only a few people talking about it, the issue never gets discussed. It's a slow-building process that starts from the bottom.

This bottom-up approach mirrors the message observed earlier in coming home narratives: change happens through a process of education of ordinary citizens, with the goal of normalizing an issue without intervention from above. Such an approach avoids direct confrontation and emphasizes harmony over dissent. This is in line with a harmony-centered approach, and it speaks to the wide-ranging and sometimes contradictory power of this cultural concept. Harmony (and harmonious behavior) grounds discourses in the cultural context of family and state-society relationships, but it has also been used by the state itself as an effective tool of social control (Lei 2018).

Harmony, Quality, and Belonging: Risks and Opportunities of a Harmonious Identity

This chapter has shown how PFLAG organizers and participants present the objective of the group as in line with the grand project of a harmonious society, and has explored the process of identity building within the group as one that privileges family—and by extension so-cial—belonging as the main characteristics uniting young tongzhi. Through narrative strategies such as the sharing of coming home sto-ries, PFLAG mobilizes the language of harmony to displace a political project of tongzhi visibility into a natural process of understanding and acceptance, and by so doing, it eases the tension between valued cul-tural traditions and potentially disruptive change.

The notion of social belonging, so central to the identity of the group, should not be left unchallenged. As a group, PFLAG contributes to the creation of a particular ideal-type of tongzhi subject—an individual who deserves inclusion into the category of Chinese citizen due to their contribution to society, social harmony, and progress. This idealized tongzhi subject embodies characteristics of a "high quality" (*gao suzhi*) citizen in the eyes of the state. The rhetoric of *suzhi* (quality) has been particularly dear to the Chinese state since the 1980s, both as a driving force in the process of modernization and economic growth and as a rhetorical tool for social control, meant to crystallize social hierarchies through the production of an ideal citizen that is urban, middle-class, educated, and socially responsible (Bao 2018; Jacka 2009; Tomba 2009). In the context of the tongzhi community, the rhetoric of suzhi perpetu-ates social exclusions across the rural-urban divide, and reinforces a bi-nary distinction between a "bad tongzhi" (scarcely educated, hyper-sexual, and low quality) and a "good tongzhi" (educated, desexualized, and high quality) (Bao 2018; L. Ho 2009; Kong 2010; Rofel 2007).

While the specific language of suzhi did not appear often in PFLAG's materials and during official events, the group is very explicitly con-cerned with a creation of a "high quality" environment. This was par-ticularly evident in the way chat room behavior was policed—erotic texts and images were explicitly prohibited, and members were reprimanded for soliciting hook-ups and discussing topics deemed too sexual. This was often justified by drawing on a distinction between public and pri-vate behavior, such as in these messages shared by an administrator on a popular WeChat group created after an event on the cruise ship:

> Many male tongzhi have a poor sense of boundaries. I don't know why, but they like to post naked pictures when they enter the group chat.

These groups are public spaces. It is important to draw a distinction between public space and private space.

The notion that sexual behavior should be policed and confined to the realm of the private is not novel, but in the case of PFLAG, this separation was particularly central because of the presence of parents. Both online and offline, desexualizing the tongzhi identity and shielding parents from their children's sexual desires seemed key to maintaining harmony. The group's coming home stories, as this chapter has explored, primarily focus on behaviors and moral characteristics that eliminate frictions, promote harmony, and present tongzhi as respectable citizens and filial sons and daughters worthy of social belonging. Many of the indirect strategies young tongzhi use for coming out also reflect a concern with quality—Lucetta Kam (2013, 99) called it a "two step model to coming out: first, to stand up as a 'model' member of society, and then, to come out as a 'less desirable' sexual being."

The risk embedded in this narrative strategy is that of reinforcing a single success story, one where the ideal tongzhi embodies the same characteristics that grant belonging to the heteronormative subject: a good relationship with their parents, a desire for a stable and monogamous romantic relationship with their partner, and other normative markers of success such as economic stability and academic achievements. In other words, PFLAG's push for tongzhi social belonging through the lens of harmony risks elevating and crystalizing a kind of homonormative sexual subject that leaves little room for other notions or embodiments of queerness—something that sexuality scholars would recognize as "a particular modality of sexual citizenship, one that is privatized, 'de-politicised,' 'de-eroticised,' and domesticated" (Richardson 2017, 213). In fact, the image of the "ideal tongzhi" that appears in many PFLAG promotional materials, including the short film that opened this chapter, could be seen as mirroring the kind of sexual politics that Lisa Duggan (2002, 179) termed "the new homonormativity—a politics that does not contest dominant heteronormative assumptions and institutions, but upholds and sustains them." At the same time, however, PFLAG's focus on this civil, politically and socially nonthreatening tongzhi subject should also be read in the political context of contemporary China as deliberate and strategic and as a central component of the organization's discursive strategy to gain visibility and promote social change.

Cultural concepts such as harmony and filial piety should then be approached with caution, as potentially double-edged: they both anchor and constrain the development of tongzhi discourses within PFLAG, and they can simultaneously signal social belonging while resulting in new exclusions. Keeping this complexity in mind, the next chapter explores how reliance on these concepts opens up possibilities for political intervention. The chapter analyzes two instances of PFLAG organizers taking advantage of such possibilities and shows how harmony is used strategically as a means to push the boundaries of noncontentiousness.

3

Rainbow Umbrellas and Wedding *Qipao*

Pushing the Limits of Contention

O n any given Saturday in Shanghai, parents flock to the centrally located Renmin Park armed with umbrellas, papers, and pieces of string to participate in a large "marriage market," hoping to find a suitable match for their son or daughter. Pieces of paper—containing vital information about the potential match—are tied with string or tape to open umbrellas, and passersby can browse around the park like they would at a farmers market. Paper postings usually list age, height, weight, zodiac sign, birthplace, job, and major achievements as well as a few words about what the family and the individual are looking for in a partner.

On the early morning of May 20, 2017, the park was especially packed because the date marks Lovers' Day in China, a particularly auspicious day for a match.[1] Among many somber-colored umbrellas, a line of large, brightly colored rainbow umbrellas started attracting the attention of the crowd. Confused passersby would soon start asking questions to the owners of those curious umbrellas—twelve mothers with some unusual-looking postings—and before the end of the morning, lively chatter would turn into angry shouting and all the rainbow umbrellas and their owners would be unceremoniously removed from the park by security. The forcible removal of mothers from Renmin Park marked the end of what members of the tongzhi community now simply refer to as "520," a semiautonomous activity organized by twelve PFLAG mothers, a few young volunteers from the organization's Shanghai branch, and the local lesbian dating app ReLa. The purpose of the activity was to raise awareness and increase positive tongzhi visibility, but the harsh response from security transformed it into a cautionary tale whispered among tongzhi volunteers and organizers.

While I expected the controversy around the Renmin Park action to lead to a cooling off of public tongzhi actions, I was wrong. Less than a month after 520, many of those same mothers and volunteers who had carried rainbow umbrellas stood on the deck of a cruise ship celebrating the first same-sex collective wedding ceremony organized by a tongzhi group in the PRC. Just like the 520 event, the wedding ceremony focused on raising tongzhi visibility by emphasizing parental approval of, and involvement in, their children's romantic lives. The unfolding and outcome of the wedding, however, stands in stark contrast with the matchmaking event: despite the public and potentially contentious nature of both performances, the wedding encountered little resistance and ultimately became PFLAG's most successful and daring celebration of tongzhi existence in the PRC.

In Chapter 2, I showed how the language of family belonging allows PFLAG to depoliticize tongzhi identity by displacing the political into the familial and by promoting tongzhi social belonging through their visible existence within their family. Here, I look at the ways this downplaying of the political is—paradoxically—a key strategy PFLAG relies on to support the political project of tongzhi visibility and social inclusion. I rely on a comparison of the two aforementioned events— the successful wedding ceremony, and the less successful 520 event—to analyze under which conditions activists are effective in lowering the perceived political contentiousness of activities and under which circumstances their actions fail. In particular, I focus on three elements that, I argue, played a particularly pivotal role in tipping the scale toward or away from political contentiousness: space, performance, and alignment to state discourses.

Out of the Park, Under the Stars: Navigating the Politics of Space

The marriage market event took place in a physical location rich with political symbolism. Renmin Park is an important historical landmark in Shanghai, and its significance is tightly connected to the political history of the city. The park was once a horse racetrack, the Shanghai Race Club, founded by the British in 1862 during the occupation of Shanghai in the midst of the Taiping Rebellion. In 1933, the club building (now the Shanghai Art Museum) was added to the track, one of its prominent features being a flagpole made from the mast of a Chinese warship captured by U.K. and U.S. troops (You and He, 2004). On October 1, 1949, when the CCP founded the People's Republic of China, people in the city reclaimed the flagpole by using it to hang the new Chinese national flag. The newly established government banned gambling activities across China, and in 1952, the racecourse was converted into Renmin Park and Renmin Square (the northern and southern parts of the old racecourse, respectively). The area would once again become politically salient in the late '80s, at the height of student unrest in China. In December 1986, tens of thousands of students gathered in Renmin Square to ask for democratization, marching together toward The Bund.[2] On December 22, the third day of protest, the Communist Party chief of Shanghai Jiang Zemin met with the students and started a six-hour-long conversation in which demonstrators asked for "democracy, recognition of their movement as nationalistic and correct, no recrimination against students who participated, and freedom of the press" (Kwong 1988, 979).

Historically, Renmin Square and the adjacent Renmin Park have been a significant arena for the creation and contestation of political meaning. In today's China, the park maintains its historical significance while also being a central part of everyday life in the city. As the most centrally located public park in Shanghai, it is a favorite tourist destination and a treasured site for locals. For participants in PFLAG's 520 event, taking up space in the park was a central part of the intended message. In one of my conversations with Dove, a twenty-seven-year-old event participant and a volunteer in PFLAG Shanghai, he explained that the event had less to do with matchmaking and more with the right to be part of the park as a social space:

> This was an activity for visibility, like [in English] *advertising*. That is to say, if heterosexuals can have public matchmaking, why can't we as homosexuals? In this sense, the park is actually under occupation by heterosexuality, there is no room for us.

Given the history of the park, Dove's reference to occupation is particularly significant. As a public space where heterosexual families can stand in the spotlight weekend after weekend, Dove saw the park as a perfect setting to normalize the existence of homosexual relationships and to reclaim tongzhi belonging. At the same time, the public location of the event turned out to be central to its downfall—when local authorities arrived at the scene, they were able to justify their intervention by claiming the event was a commercial activity, which would require a special authorization to be carried out in a public place. Furthermore, the openness to the public exposed participants to the possibility of negative public reception, especially since the marriage market is considered a location frequented by relatively conservative, "traditional" parents.

The cruise wedding, on the contrary, took place in a semiprivate space, in the context of PFLAG's annual kentanhui on a ship owned by a Chinese company. Initially, PFLAG organizers had planned for the event to take place in a completely private setting, and they had selected a 1,200-passenger ship that they had booked in full. This was marketed as a central feature of the event and emphasized in promotional material and messages. For example, PFLAG's executive director Ah Qiang publicized the cruise as such in one of the early posts about the cruise: "The whole ship will be tongzhi and their families, so prejudice and discrimination won't get in the way" (WeChat post, December 12, 2016). In the original plan, the cruise destination was to be Jeju Island (Korea), a four-day, three-night round trip. Ah Qiang and other organizers worked tirelessly for months in order to set up a reservation system and to raise enough funds through donations and sponsorships.[3]

In early 2017, however, international tensions forced PFLAG to re-think its plans: South Korea's decision to allow the United States to de-ploy a Terminal High Altitude Area Defense System (THAAD) on its soil angered China, and amid rising tensions, the Chinese government reinstituted a ban on mainland tour groups traveling to South Korea. As a result of the situation, PFLAG had to reenvision its summer ken-tanhui and opted for a longer cruise (five days, four nights) to Japan. The change came with a host of new challenges: the additional length caused problems for those who had already put in requests for vacation days at work, and the new itinerary caused an increase in costs of over CNY 200 (~US$30) per person. The new plan also forced PFLAG to join a route for which a few hundred tickets had already been sold, which meant that participants would have to share the space with a number of unaffiliated passengers. For all these late changes, unexpected ob-stacles, and consequent cancellations, however, tickets for the kentan-hui were all sold out by early May, with over eight hundred expected participants from all parts of China.

Despite the semiprivate and commercial nature of the location, the collective wedding was by no means shielded from official scrutiny. During the boarding process, Ah Qiang was questioned by local po-lice, and there was an unconfirmed rumor going around of someone being taken off the boat by customs police under "suspicion of abnor-mal behavior." When I discussed the events with Ah Qiang after the cruise was over, he minimized the situation by explaining that the only official worry concerned my presence and that of a documentary film crew from the Netherlands:

> You know, when we were boarding the ship, a policeman asked me to . . . he talked to me for more than twenty minutes. But the only question he had, well, this policeman saw some foreign-ers joining our cruise, so he just wanted to know what they were doing on board. [*Gestures toward me.*] But your background is uncomplicated. You are not a foreign power.

Ah Qiang was able to dispel any worries about my status relying on both my nationality—as an Italian citizen, I was nonthreatening on a glob-al scale—and my status as a student.[4] These small tensions aside, the boarding process and the opening ceremony on June 14 happened smoothly and without any notable incidents. The following night, however, on the evening of the much-awaited collective wedding, space suddenly became problematic. The ceremony had been planned as an indoor event, to happen in the largest hall on the cruise ship—the same space where all other events had taken place. The event was scheduled to start at 8:00 P.M., and by 6:30, everyone was there. The hall was packed, all seats taken and every square inch of available floor space occupied. The excitement was palpable, everyone talking loudly and waving rainbow flags. All the commotion died down as soon as the music started and the lights went off. Behind the stage, a bright red screen displayed the character 囍 *xi*, a traditional ornament used during wedding ceremonies.[5] Couples entered the hall and introduced themselves and their families on stage, cheered and encouraged by the public. After the introductions were over, one of the organizers jumped on stage and made an unexpected announcement: "OK, now everyone stand up. The first part of the ceremony happened here, but for the rest of it, we will go to up the main deck, OK? Let's go, let's give them a ceremony at sea."

Everyone in the hall was terribly confused by the announcement—nowhere in the program did it say anything about the ceremony happening under the stars. After a few moments of puzzlement, eight hundred people slowly made their way toward the upstairs deck, where another unexpected request awaited. Due to last-minute changes, no one but authorized PFLAG personnel would be able to photograph or video record the wedding. In the general excitement of the ceremony, participants shrugged off the unusual nature of the requirement and mostly complied with the instructions. The ceremony under the stars continued until late at night and was followed by spontaneous dancing, singing, and celebratory toasts all around.

The day after the wedding, some of the organizers explained to me that the location change had been dictated by the captain and that they were informed of the requested move ten minutes into the event. The captain feared the cruise company would not approve of photographs being taken inside, in the easily recognizable sixth-floor hall. Indeed, the photograph that came to symbolize the successful wedding ceremony is one where the nine couples stand on a wooden deck that could be anywhere in the world: the background is pitch black, the sea completely invisible. The photograph made tongzhi history, and it is also an uncannily accurate representation of the spatial positionality that allowed the ceremony to happen at all. The nine couples stand in a liminal position: in international waters, standing between an invisible sea and stars, surrounded by nothing but a nondescript wooden floor. At the same time, as I explore in more detail in a later section, the nine couples are also unequivocally located in China, performing a traditional Chinese wedding ceremony. Surrounded by darkness, they are simultaneously removed from, and solidly grounded within, the PRC.

Participants' interaction with physical space is an element that clearly differentiates the collective wedding from the marriage market event. Undeniably, the location of the wedding ceremony meant the event did not happen in the public eye. In terms of taking up space, 520 was quite arguably bolder, louder, and more explicit in its political purpose. The physical reclamation of a heterosexual space, however, came at a steep price—the abrupt interruption of the event, the threat of arrest for those involved, and the risk for the organization to be labeled a potential social threat. By labeling the event a commercial activity, park security was able to leverage the location of 520 as an official reason to expel participants. Their presence in the park, however, is not the reason why authorities were called in the first place. As I show in the next section, the initial motivation for police intervention appears to be less connected with space and more with what participants were doing in the park— their public performance.

Performing Harmony and Tradition

Both 520 and the collective wedding were planned—to a certain extent even choreographed—performative acts. Both were meant to signal tongzhi demands for inclusion within two cultural arenas—matchmaking in one case, marriage in the other. In both events, participants disrupted and reenvisioned a socially defined "normal" by making tongzhi existence visible in strictly heterosexual cultural contexts. When talking about Renmin Park, participating mothers addressed visible disruption of the norm as a central goal of the activity. Fire Mama, a volunteer from Hangzhou who traveled to Shanghai for the event, explained to me during a lunch conversation that the confusion initially caused by the PFLAG mothers' presence in the park had given rise to fruitful conversations with perplexed passersby:

> It was even fun at first. People came to us and said: "You wrote your sign wrong, you got the characters mixed up![6] It looks like you're looking for a girl for your daughter," and we explained that there was no mistake, that our children were homosexuals. And people were listening, there was no problem.

Here, Fire Mama was describing the first few hours of 520, in which she and other mothers had discreetly occupied a corner of the park and had simply waited for other parents to show up and notice the unusual search criteria displayed on their signs. As she continued with her story, she explained she could pinpoint the precise moment things started to go sour:

> The problems began with the logo. We put the PFLAG logo and the ReLa logo on display, and that attracted more attention and people started saying: "Ah, what is this logo? Why are you here?" If we hadn't opened the rainbow umbrellas and we hadn't put the banners on display, it would have been fine. Before we did that, we were just some moms there to find a partner for their children. If mothers of heterosexual kids can do it, why not us?

In her recounting of the events of the day, the switch from dark-colored to rainbow umbrellas and the conspicuous display of two banners with the PFLAG logo had an almost instantaneous effect. Importantly, while the display contributed in making them more visible, Fire Mama hints at something more subtle. As mothers, they were visible *before* the banners and the umbrellas. But that was the key—they were visible *as mothers*. As soon as those came out, though, they stopped being "just some moms" and became something else. Dove also had a strikingly similar recollection:

> And it was at eight o'clock, when there were more and more people, we replaced the umbrellas with rainbow umbrellas, and then

everyone started getting upset. There was no problem until then, *but at that point it became advocacy* [emphasis mine].

Dove and Fire Mama are both singling out the moment in which the mothers' actions and readable behavior transitioned from acceptable (mothers looking out for their children) to unacceptable (activists engaging in advocacy). Video recordings from the day capture the transition in even sharper detail, as they show the group of mothers leaving the matchmaking corner and reaching into their backpacks to take out large signs. These signs, bright red Chinese characters on a white background, displayed a variety of slogans ranging from "Support tongzhi, oppose discrimination" to "True love knows no gender, support a son looking for a boyfriend" and "ReLa supports families who bravely speak out." Some of them were in English, reading "Keep calm, it's just love" and "I love my gay daughter and her future wife." Visually, the performance was unambiguously confrontational compared to the earlier portion of the event. Mothers started walking through the park holding the signs over their heads, followed by a few younger participants who were recording everything on their phones. The signs themselves suggested an oppositional stance, both in their content and their appearance—the large characters on plain background reminiscent of *dazibao*, "big character posters," which have been part of the historical repertoire of political protest in China since the 1911 revolution. When park security arrived at the scene, they immediately confiscated the signs and handed them to the police.

In many ways, the banner action on 520 was an unusual activity for PFLAG. While tongzhi mothers' presence in the park fit the narrative of social belonging that the group so adamantly emphasizes, their performance did not. By displaying their signs and parading around the park, 520 participants crossed the invisible line of noncontentiousness—they ceased to be "like other mothers" and instead became political, contentious, nonbelonging.

The collective wedding ceremony had a similar potential—if not greater—for becoming a contentious event. The organizing of the ceremony was characterized by debates over potential risks and obstacles, and worries were exacerbated by the timing of the event: 520 had been abruptly cut short less than a month earlier, in the same city where the cruise was set to depart; to add to this, a few weeks prior to the wedding, on May 24, the Constitutional Court of Taiwan had ruled the ban on same-sex marriage unconstitutional, paving the way for its legalization in the country. This contributed to raising the potential for contention, and PFLAG organizers worried about the possibility of going through with the plan. Ah Qiang acknowledged the many difficulties, and shared his uncertainties in a blog post published shortly after the ceremony:

> As we started planning the collective wedding of ten tongzhi couples, I was very hesitant. In circumstances where there's no legal protection, can we really give these loving tongzhi couples a ceremony? And what type of ceremony would meet the needs of these tongzhi couples, but also highlight the image of Chinese tongzhi?

Ah Qiang's post points at two potential issues that organizers were considering during the planning phase: On one side, the ceremony came with certain safety concerns, as PFLAG could not guarantee any legal protection to the couples involved in the event. On the other side, PFLAG leadership was also worried about the message the wedding ceremony would send. During one of our conversations, I asked Ah Qiang about the post and the importance of reflecting a *Chinese* image of the tongzhi community. His answer pointed to the strategic implications of making the ceremony a performance of cultural belonging:

> I think this was first and foremost an epoch-making event. And the other thing is, at the same time we are saying, OK, a Chinese wedding ceremony won't create a problem, because we don't want to give other people the impression that this is influenced by foreign forces. We are homosexuals living within Chinese culture, and [these nine couples],[7] they want to get married too, right?

Ah Qiang was hinting at the risk of creating an event that would appear to "mimic" collective weddings in other countries—turning the celebration into an item on a global (foreign-influenced) LGBT movement checklist. In order to avoid that outcome, PFLAG organizers decided to put together a performance that would clearly reflect and celebrate Chinese culture. This entailed coordinating a carefully choreographed spectacle, every component of which paid tribute to various elements of Chinese tradition. Organizers planned every detail, from music to the couples' outfits to—most importantly—the central role played by parents during the wedding.

On the day of the ceremony, as lights went out and the character 囍 was projected on the bright red screen, the nine couples entered the stage in a slow procession, coordinating their steps to match the background music. Each couple was wearing a matching outfit, a red or blue *qipao* (or a qipao jacket) with golden accents.[8] In line with PFLAG's signature strategy, parents were invited on stage to show their support for the children. After each couple briefly introduced themselves, the host of the ceremony shifted the focus of attention onto the parents:

> HOST: I believe that for a tongzhi, the happiest thing is to get the support of parents and family. Today, some of these couples' family members are present here. We have invited them on stage to share the happiness of their children. OK, I want to ask a few parents . . . I want to ask parents a few questions. Coal Mama, why do you support your child in such a wedding?
>
> COAL MAMA: Every parent wants to see their child happy and attend their wedding. This is what I most hope for. It doesn't matter whether my child is homosexual or heterosexual, as long as he finds his other half and is in love, he has my blessing. I wish them a long happiness.

Coal Mama's answer was a typical one, as other parents after her went through a round of similar statements about their support for the ceremony. Through this prearranged public interaction, parents became the de facto conveyors of tongzhi demands, a strategy in line with PFLAG's usual modus operandi. In this case, once again, the political (a demand for marriage rights) was displaced into the familial (the culturally resonant hope of every Chinese parent to see their child get married).

The presence of parents on the stage was deemed so important for the success of the event that during the planning phase, PFLAG leaders made it a strict requirement for any couple who wished to take part in the ceremony. Ah Qiang articulated this as a key strategic move during one of our interviews:

> So we said, "If you want to be part of the wedding, you need at least one family member that has to be able to attend." Of course, if more than one come, that's even better, right? Because we think that this signals that our wedding has been recognized by relatives. . . . Because we are a public welfare organization, we are not engaging in recreational activities. The way we do this thing, we do it with some sense of advocacy. So now let's say you plan to be part of the same-sex wedding. But then you are doing that sneakily, your parents do not know, there is no one there to support you, this seems a bit distasteful, you know? Then it seems very lonely, or it feels as if you are not being accepted.

The wedding ceremony was thus carefully crafted to be a celebration of tongzhi love but also and especially a representation of tongzhi acceptance within the family. The couples' performance revolved around their parents, and as the ceremony reached its climax with the exchange of the rings, the host directed the couples to perform three bows. Traditionally, couples first bow to heaven and earth, then to their parents, and finally to each other. In this case, however, couples were instructed to bow three times to their parents: "Now face your parents. Do a first bow, to thank your parents for their support. Now a second one, to wish your parents good health. And a third one, your family must be a complete and united family. Now please sit down with your parents." At this point, parents on stage also gave their children traditional red envelopes—monetary gifts that signify parental approval of the union.

Despite the timing and the inherently political nature of a same-sex wedding ceremony being celebrated in a country where same-sex weddings are not legal, any reference to civil rights was notably absent from the cruise event. Participants performed following the rules of Chinese tradition, and the event was hailed as a celebration of family love, acceptance, and social harmony. Through a carefully depoliticized performance, participants in the event were able to avoid crossing the boundary of the political—the invisible line that just a few weeks prior transformed the twelve 520 mothers into activists.

Importantly, the collective wedding's success was not limited to the fact that the event was allowed to happen without any major incidents: as soon as the ceremony was over, photographs and articles describing the event went viral on WeChat and started populating tongzhi group chats all over the country. Reporters on the cruise covered the event, and on the day the ship returned to Shanghai, the *South China Morning Post* published a featured article titled "The Love Boat" that detailed the events of the cruise and focused particularly on the wedding ceremony.[9] Articles appeared in online newspapers in both English and Chinese, without encountering resistance or censorship. The wedding photo remained the central feature on the front page of PFLAG's public website well into 2019, featured prominently years after the event. In contrast, after the twelve mothers were kicked out of Renmin Park on 520, news of the altercations circulated among tongzhi groups and members of the community, but videos and articles were quickly removed from social media. Tongzhi groups, including PFLAG, scrambled to remove any reference to the event from their pages for fear of having their accounts blocked or removed. The event was rendered virtually invisible, and removed from most Chinese-language media. The lesbian dating app ReLa, which had co-organized the event, was contacted by the Cyberspace Administration of China (CAC) and asked to remove all content related to the event from video sharing sites. A few days later, the app was completely shut down and all their previously published content removed from the web.

"What PFLAG Is About": Strategic Alignment with State Discourse

Both 520 and the collective wedding ceremony were activities designed for visibility, and both relied on a similar strategic approach—mothers of tongzhi advocating for their children and voicing political demands on their behalf. What differentiated the two events was how they were read in political terms: 520 was read as activism in a central, urban, politicized location, while the wedding was read as a celebration of family ties in a semiprivate, liminal space. The success and public visibility of the wedding and the virtual erasure of 520 shed light on a key element that informs PFLAG's strategy and that seems to be reflected in the two drastically different outcomes: the group's ability to connect their work and their existence as an organization to a government-approved vision of China's future.

On May 31, eleven days after 520 and two weeks before the cruise, Ah Qiang published an article on his public WeChat account, in which he clarified PFLAG's mission and vision for the future:

> PFLAG's work has been dedicated to promoting family and social harmony by improving family acceptance and sharing the same concerns as the government and society. Our work has been recognized by some officials in different cities on different occasions. However, the situation has changed a little recently. The work of the tongzhi community has been interpreted by a minority of prejudiced people as "causing social instability" and "an ideological problem." Obviously, this is an incorrect interpretation.

Ah Qiang's wording and rhetorical choices are dense with political implications. While he doesn't directly reference 520, his mention of tongzhi groups being unjustly accused of causing social instability is an allusion to the aftermath of the Shanghai event. He strategically mobilizes the language of social harmony and explicitly draws a connection between PFLAG's work and the official stance of government officials in various cities. As discussed in the previous chapter, the strategic appeal to a harmony-based rhetoric allows the organization to claim political belonging by emphasizing alignment with the government-promoted goal of a "harmonious society."

Ah Qiang's choice to emphasize stability should also be contextualized within the increasingly treacherous political environment in which grassroots groups like PFLAG operate. The steadily increasing friction between the CCP and grassroots organizations is reflected in the ubiquitous presence of a state-promoted discourse depicting public opinion as "an increasingly negative influence on the harmony of Chinese society" (Lei 2018, 29). Crackdowns on contention have steadily intensi-

fied under the leadership of President Xi Jinping, with an increased tar-
geting of groups mobilizing in defense or support of rights (ibid., 31).
By showing PFLAG's alignment with state discourses, and by distancing the group's work from rights-based advocacy, Ah Qiang's post aims
to remove any connection between the organization and (potential) social disruption. Showing this strategy, he goes on to mobilize another
politically salient discourse:

> The tongzhi community is more active than ever, which shows
> that our society has become more civilized, more inclusive, and
> most of all, it reflects China's great progress, and China's soft
> power. . . . I hope that the living conditions of Chinese tongzhi
> can be a leading example for the world.

Here, Ah Qiang reframes the political work of tongzhi groups in a light
that favors China's global standing, suggesting that the inclusion and
acceptance of sexual minorities could potentially give the country an
edge over foreign powers. His choice of words is once again strategic:
he mobilizes the concept of *wenming* (civility), a rhetorical staple often
used by the Chinese state together in close connection with the term
suzhi (quality) that was discussed at the end of Chapter 2. In particular, "*wenming shehui*, literally 'civilized society,' has been . . . adopted
by the party-state to indicate the civilizing role of its governance" (De
Seta 2018, 2016). By appropriating and repurposing state rhetoric, Ah
Qiang makes the case for the civilizing power of tongzhi visibility—
welcoming tongzhi into Chinese society as worthy citizens, he implies,
is a step toward achieving the state goal of a modern, civilized society.

Ah Qiang's rhetoric of civility and soft power requires a careful balancing act. Taken without context, his words could easily be read as a
kind of homonationalist rhetoric—that is, an approach where "the right
to, or quality of sovereignty is . . . evaluated by how a nation treats its
homosexuals" (Puar and Mikdashi 2012). This kind of rhetoric has been
discussed as a strategy used by hegemonic powers (particularly the United States, in the original formulation of the term) to justify their neo-
colonial project through a strategic othering of nations and cultures
deemed "sexually backward" for their treatment of sexual minorities
(Puar 2007, 2011; Schotten 2016). In Ah Qiang's post, however, this

project is absent—the accusation of being sexually backward is directed to the China of the past, as a way to emphasize the achievements of the present. As if to guard against a potential reading of his words as too close to an idolizing of an abstract (Western) neoliberal project, a few paragraphs later he adds that "homosexuality is not the decadent lifestyle of the bourgeoisie." This discursive approach is especially significant as it complicates existing paradigms of transnational sexual identity politics—while existing research suggests that groups and individuals articulate hybrid sexual identities by combining local traditions and Western models (Boellstorff 2005; Carrillo 1999), PFLAG's approach points to an explicit localizing of the tongzhi community as a strategic tool for political survival.

Looking at 520 and the collective wedding ceremony, it becomes clear that only one of the two events succeeded at being perceived as an example of China's movement toward a local, unequivocally Chinese version of modernity. When the twelve Shanghai mothers were challenged by passersby in the park, they had to respond to two different strands of criticism, both equally damning: on one side, they were critiqued for turning a peaceful matchmaking activity into a disruptive, protest-like performance; on the other side, they also faced online ridicule for their choice of activity. When news of the event initially spread online, young netizens (both tongzhi and nontongzhi) started ridiculing it for being "backward," as participants were seemingly asking for tongzhi inclusion in matchmaking—an activity that is considered embarrassing and antiquated by most Chinese citizens who consider themselves "modern." Dove explained to me that this reaction caught participants by surprise:

> On Weibo, the online discussion turned out to be different from what we had imagined. People were saying that one should not marry someone they had never met before. That is, whether one has come out or not, before getting married one should meet and get to know a partner.

Other participants were equally dismayed by the fact that online observers had taken their demands so literally. Most of the mothers I talked to adamantly refuted those interpretations, and often stressed that they did not actually want to find partners for their children through the marriage market. Sapphire Mama, a mother of two and a part-time volunteer in the Shanghai PFLAG branch, clarified that "[PFLAG mothers] don't actually interfere with their children's marriage; they can do it themselves."

At the same time, 520 participants were criticized for being too forward, too close to activism, "too Western." Their use of English-language signs was interpreted as a move to attract the attention of Western media, which would put China in a negative light in the foreign press. In one of the few Chinese-language articles still available online, the author writes:

> From what we understand, one of the parent volunteers spoke to the media in English, saying: "We are (tongzhi) mothers, my son is gay, my daughter is a lesbian." At the scene, other parents did not understand. Some condemned the tongzhi parents: "What they are doing here is illegal! They are liars." After the tongzhi parents set up shop, a man said: "Gay issues should not enter the public eye, their choices are wrong, they violate Chinese traditional values!"[10]

Paradoxically, then, 520 ended up being criticized for being simultaneously too tied to traditional behavior and too disrespectful of traditional values. Nothing about the activity could be promoted as harmonious—the parents disrupted everyday activities in the park, and the idea of tongzhi blind dates had the potential to embarrass tongzhi youth and create a fracture between them and their parents.

By contrast, the collective wedding ceremony balanced traditional elements deemed important for a contemporary Chinese national identity—through an emphasis on marriage as a celebration of family ties—with modern notions of romantic love that centered on couples celebrating their "pure love." The lavish cruise setting also contributed to present a picture of modern China that is cosmopolitan, that celebrates international exchange (while remaining anchored to its history and traditions), and that glorifies leisure. In a widely quoted article that was published in full on several online websites and newspapers, a member of PFLAG presented the cruise and the wedding ceremony as follows:

In the magnificent East China Sea, the cruise ship hosting the Tenth National PFLAG kentanhui sails among the waves; and on the deep and vast sea of love, the sweet boat will raise its love sails on the night of June 15, 2017. Here, beautiful dreams are about to become a reality, beautiful lives are about to open a new chapter, nine new families will get their happy ending with 800 other members of a sexual minority group and their relatives and friends as their witness. This evening, with love as our paper and affinity as our pen, we write happiness together. . . .

If our wedding celebration was full of happiness and warmth, it is because of the hundreds of tongzhi and relatives who were here to witness it. Thanks to the sincere blessings of the parents and friends present here, happiness and peace will always accompany the life of these newlyweds.

As a celebration of love and family support, the wedding ceremony, while unprecedented in scale, was able to stay within an acceptable, nonpolitical framework—applauding family unity without explicitly asking for political change. The celebration of Chinese culture and the forward-looking vision it presented made the event palatable both within and outside the tongzhi community. In an article circulated on multiple news media platforms and titled "A special wedding on board,"[11] the author walked readers through the evening of the wedding, reporting the emotional words of parents declaring that their son's partner is "just the same as acquiring a daughter-in-law." The author also commented on the overarching mood before embarking the ship: "Boarding hasn't started yet, but the journey of homosexuals and their families has already begun. There is nothing weird about it, everyone seems happy and relaxed." The normalizing narrative serves groups like PFLAG well, by emphasizing their belonging in society as regular families and citizens.

For PFLAG, the wedding was also a successful test of which strategic approach could allow the group to organize large-scale events despite their potential political contentiousness. In the days following the collective ceremony, I witnessed multiple conversations that revolved around the success of the event and that praised PFLAG leaders' approach to planning and advertising it. Given the recent news from Taiwan, I often asked participants whether they imagined China moving in a similar direction in regard to legalizing same-sex marriage. During a dinner conversation with Maple Baba, the father of a young PFLAG volunteer from Xi'an, he explained what he saw as the secret for successful tongzhi organizing in the PRC:

> Taiwan has a Pride Parade every year, but you won't see this in China. Are you familiar with Laozi? 上善若水 [*shang shan ruo shui*, "all good deeds are like water," or "the highest good is like water"]. You don't play with water. It keeps the boat afloat, but it can also capsize it.

Maple Baba's words spoke of the success of the wedding ceremony, but they also frame the capsizing of 520. The idea of "not playing with water" encapsulates PFLAG's challenging position between stability and contention as the group strives to navigate an unsteady political environment. While both the 520 action and the wedding ceremony centered on parents demanding inclusion on behalf of their tongzhi children, only the latter could be discursively aligned to a state-promoted vision of a modern China, forward-looking and yet respectful of traditions, cosmopolitan and yet proudly Chinese, demanding of change and yet focused on social harmony. And while the 2017 collective ceremony currently remains the largest and most daring activity organized by the PFLAG, the strategic approach of mirroring state-promoted discourses has kept PFLAG afloat and allowed the organization to thrive in the face of heightened governmental scrutiny directed toward civil society groups.

Not Playing with Water: Rhetorical Strategies for Public Visibility

As a group whose declared goal is to improve tongzhi social acceptance, PFLAG measures success in terms of positive visibility—and they are especially attentive to opportunities for media coverage. Creek, the older PFLAG organizer who had been part of the original core group when it was founded in 2008, explained to me during an interview that the group always puts a premium on organizing events that can be easily translated into positive news stories within the PRC:

> Because we do it, of course, with our purpose, because we want to raise the visibility of the community. We all know the importance of visibility! Serving the people is a very important job of PFLAG, but on another level, on a social advocacy level, raising visibility is very important. . . . We have a lot of cooperation with the media, even with the Chinese media, although we understand they are state controlled.

Creek's remarks acknowledge the importance of family-focused events for community-building purposes but also underline the strategic political meaning of such emphasis. Alignment with state discourses as a rhetorical strategy requires the group to maintain a certain degree of flexibility, and a continuous discursive reinvention of their goals. By continuously and purposefully avoiding contention—by choosing over and over not to play with water—PFLAG has been able to minimize the potentially negative impact of governmental crackdowns that have left other grassroots groups scrambling. The summer of 2017 provides an example of the strategic value of this approach.

At the end of June 2017, a few weeks after the wedding ceremony, the Chinese government started a nationwide crackdown on virtual private network (VPN) services, effectively stopping individuals from bypassing the "Great Firewall of China" to access uncensored websites. As governmental scrutiny increased, the PFLAG headquarters asked local groups to include the following slogan on all flyers advertising public events: "Promoting family harmony, promoting mutual love among relatives, promoting the healthy growth of the next generation, ensuring the elderly will be properly cared for." While the slogan is paired with the organization's logo and name—which unequivocally reference homosexuality—sexual identity is seemingly erased in this public presentation of the group's goals. Harmony and family stability continue to occupy a privileged position but are now paired with new elements: growth, economic security, and social and financial stability for both the new and old generation. All these are elements that purposely reflect Xi Jinping's political narrative of a nationalistic Chinese Dream—

which emphasizes history, culture, and patriotism and aligns the dream of a strong nation with issues of central importance to the general public, such as financial stability and access to public health and housing (Z. Wang 2014). In the new slogan, PFLAG is thus depicted as a group that is not only working toward the same nationalist goal of strengthening society but is especially interested in caring for some of the most vulnerable social categories, the young and the elderly. In this light, the group's activities become events with minimal social costs—or even better, events fulfilling an important (and state-approved) social function.

A Traditional, Modern China

By comparing two events focused on parents' involvement in their children's romantic lives, this chapter shows that PFLAG's success is connected to the group's culturally and politically informed performance and rhetorical choices. I have argued that the success of the collective same-sex wedding ceremony is tied to the explicit downplaying of the event's political potential—which paradoxically led to its success and to an increase in the visibility of the group. By looking at 520 as an example of an unsuccessful event, I have analyzed the limits of family-centered discourse, and I have suggested that a critical element distinguishing the two events is the ability of organizers and participants to present themselves and the event as in line with a vision of a harmonious, cosmopolitan, proudly nationalistic, modern *and* traditional China.

The apparent oxymoron of traditional and modern can only be resolved by letting go of dichotomous understandings of the two terms. PFLAG's discursive strategies force us to "be reflexive about the historical legacies and cultural politics of such categories" (Kim-Puri 2005, 144), as the group's strategic choices cannot be separated from a political context where belonging to the nation-state is simultaneously tied to two kinds of performance: one of cosmopolitan, consumption-driven modernity and one of cultural belonging based on tradition. The construction of an organizational (and sexual) identity that is both traditional and modern requires PFLAG to navigate the language of multiple social structures—the state, the family, the market—and to engage in processes of cultural production that speak to the fluidity of this environment.

In the final part of this chapter, I engage with this fluidity by exploring how alignment with state discourse allows PFLAG to react to unpredictable moments of political instability, flexibly adapting in order to avoid crossing the line of political contentiousness. The next chapter engages with a strategy for change that—while still relying on public visibility as a pathway to change—moves away from a harmony-based rhetoric, going instead into the more contentious territory of policy change through rights-based advocacy.

4

Going to Court

Legal Advocacy and the Limits of Rights Discourse

In February 2014, a thirty-year-old tongzhi who goes by the pseudonym Yanzi checked into the Xinyu Piaoxiang Clinic in Chongqing to undergo "conversion therapy," a multisession combination of hypnosis, medication, and electroshock therapy designed to change his sexual orientation. He had found the clinic online, clicking on the first result appearing on Baidu—the most popular search engine in China—after a keyword search for "treatment for homosexuality" (同性恋治疗 *tongxinglian zhiliao*). Once he got to the clinic, Yanzi paid CNY 500 (~US$80) for the first hour of treatment and was brought to a small room with a sofa. The doctor made some idle conversation, asked him to relax, and then started explaining that homosexuality is abnormal and that it is easy to "contract the disease [of homosexuality]." After that, he began the hypnotherapy session and eventually asked Yanzi to think about having sex with a man. A few seconds after the doctor made that request, Yanzi received his first electric shock—so unexpected that he cried out and jumped up from the sofa in terror. The doctor explained that this was a key part of the therapy, as the shocks help patients connect feelings of fear and pain to same-sex behaviors. Yanzi was so upset that he immediately left the clinic. In March 2014, one month after his first appointment, he decided to pursue legal action and to sue both the clinic and Baidu. When the Haidian District People's Court in Beijing formally accepted his case on March 15, Yanzi became the plaintiff in the first tongzhi lawsuit in the PRC.

The lawsuit became a landmark case for the tongzhi community. Yanzi's story circulated widely in international and domestic media, and when the court delivered its verdict on December 19, a photograph of Yanzi holding a statue of Lady Justice and a rainbow flag immediately made world news.[1] The court ordered the clinic to issue a formal apology to Yanzi and to reimburse him for incurred expenses. Furthermore, the court suggested that Baidu should stop including conversion therapy advertisements in its search result—a recommendation that the search engine accepted. For tongzhi groups, it was a moment of victory and validation, especially since the Beijing court publicly ruled that—in accordance with the third edition of the *Chinese Classification of Mental Disorders* (*CCMD-3*)—homosexuality is not an illness.

There is more to Yanzi's case than initially meets the eye. In fact, the lawsuit had been planned since 2013, when Yanzi started putting together a team of tongzhi-friendly lawyers who would be willing to take the case to court. When he checked himself into the Xinyu Piaoxiang clinic, he did so with the intent to collect evidence. He recorded his therapy session, and the recording became a key piece of evidence in the trial. Yanzi is the founder of a small organization called 同志平等权益促进会 Tongzhi pingdeng quanyi cujinhui, which translates to Association for the Promotion of Tongzhi Equal Rights but also goes by the English name LGBT Rights Advocacy China. Members of the group usually used the shorthand Quancuhui, meaning "rights promotion association," to talk about the organization on social media. The group, created in 2013, connects potential plaintiffs to a network of expert lawyers and works with other tongzhi groups to ensure that cases receive as much media exposure as possible. Yangzi's case was a successful "trial run" for a new strategy for the tongzhi community to gain visibility in the public sphere and—ideally—have an impact on public policy. Since the first conversion therapy lawsuit, a handful of other cases have been brought to the attention of Chinese courts,[2] and many of them have caught the attention of international and domestic media.

This chapter looks at civil lawsuits as a strategy for change in the PRC that moves beyond a rhetoric of harmony and belonging and into the more contentious rhetorical territory of rights. I analyze a few key cases that aimed to influence public opinion and pushed for policy change in the realm of health care, education, media censorship, and workplace protection. I show the discursive and linguistic work tongzhi groups, individual plaintiffs, and their lawyers engage in to maximize their chances in the courtroom, and I look at media coverage and diffusion of the results of the cases. I highlight central discrepancies between international coverage—mostly focused on rights and policy change—and tongzhi groups' understandings of the cases as opportunities to influence public opinion and I explore the limits of the language of human rights in the context of transnational cooperation.

The First Tongzhi Lawsuit: Absence of Rights, Avoidance of Rights

Relying on legal channels as a strategy for change in the context of authoritarian law may seem like a counterproductive choice, as in an authoritarian system law is almost by definition a limiting platform for change (Fu 2018, 555). In Xi Jinping's China, reliance on legal channels and rights claims further carries a particular set of risks, as Xi's administration has taken an explicit stance against the language of rights—particularly human rights (Chao and Hsu 2018; Pils 2019; Zhou 2018). During one of our conversations, I asked Yanzi why he had chosen the courtroom as a space for tongzhi engagement. He explained his decision to try legal advocacy as a novel tactic, and particularly legal advocacy in the realm of health care, was a combination of personal and strategic reasons. On a personal level, in 2012 and 2013 the increased visibility of multiple tongzhi organizations around the country meant more and more individuals started seeking support from the growing community, which led to a higher number of stories about conversion therapy experiences being circulated among groups. On a strategic level, Yanzi explained that although legal advocacy was an unexplored area for the tongzhi movement at the time, they had other examples that they could rely on for inspiration:

In 2013, we realized there was no rights advocacy in the tong-zhi movement in China, so we thought in the movement . . . there is a lack of people who are willing to do this within the movement, so we started this organization to do things. And there is another dimension to it, because we could see that in other areas, for example disability rights or hepatitis B, in those areas legal litigation has been used as a strategy to promote certain issues. There was no such thing in the tongzhi movement, so we wanted to borrow and learn from [these other cases]. We relied on the experience of others to carry out this work.

Before founding Quancuhui, Yanzi had been working in other NGOs and had been exposed to legal litigation as a possible strategy. There was, however, a key difference separating Yanzi's first conversion therapy lawsuit and the experience of legal advocates focused on the two issues he mentioned. Both in the case of disability rights and hepatitis B, lawyers and plaintiffs could mobilize existing legal frameworks that granted protection and recognition to individuals (Fu 2012; Stein 2010; Zhao 2017; Zhao and Zhang 2018). For example, in the case of hepatitis B–related lawsuits, lawyers and plaintiffs could mobilize the 2010 Notice on Cancellation of Hepatitis B Test Items in School Admission and Employment Examination (Han et al. 2018), while for disability rights they could mobilize the 1994 Regulation on the Education of Disabled Persons (Zhao and Zhang 2018) and rely on the support of state organizations like the China Disabled Persons' Federation.

For tongzhi, no equivalent law exists as nonnormative sexual identities are not mentioned anywhere in the Chinese legal code (Chia 2019). This legal invisibility required some creative work on the part of Yanzi's legal team, who initially struggled to have the case accepted. The turning point for the case was the team's decision to follow a recommendation from a Beijing judge and file it as a "contract services dispute" (合同服务纠纷 hetong fuwu jiufen), dropping all references to homosexuality (Parkin 2018, 1249). Yanzi explained that this was also a strategy borrowed from hepatitis B cases that had been successfully filed as contract service disputes in the past. Much to everyone's surprise, at the time of final judgment, the judge changed the cause of action from a contract service dispute to a "personal dignity rights dispute," a change that Yanzi qualified as an unexpected result that far exceeded his and his team's expectations.

The absence of tongzhi rights in the legal code also required a careful articulation of the intended target of the lawsuit and of justifications for taking legal action. A focus on conversion therapy services constituted a relatively safe choice because, as Yangzi explained to me, focusing on health is "more social than doing other issues, such as marriage equality. It is easier to tell the public that homosexuality is not a disease than to discuss whether it is possible for homosexuals to marry." Moreover, centering the lawsuit on the service offered by the clinic and promoted by Baidu allowed tongzhi groups to present the case as one in which the issue at hand was one of consumer rights.

Coverage of the lawsuit posted on the official Quancuhui WeChat account defended Yanzi's choice of suing the clinic by stating the following:

> If there is evidence that Chongqing Xinyu Piaoxiang is deliberately presenting homosexuality as pathological in online ads, and thereby emphasizing the promotion of their own therapy for profit, then it is obviously a case of false advertisement, which infringes on consumers' right to know and on their right to physical health.

Focusing on specific individual rights, such as health rights or, in a later lawsuit, education rights, was an important communicative strategy for the group, as doing so allowed its members to avoid relying on the language of universal human rights. A member of Yanzi's team who briefly joined us during one of our chats explained this choice was calculated, by stating, "Of course, sometimes we mention rights, but we keep it specific. Specific rights in specific cases, and we do not wave the banner of human rights. This is an important communication strategy." In Yanzi's lawsuit, framing the case as a contract dispute motivated by an infringement of consumer rights made it possible for the legal team to instead focus on the financial loss and on the health risks of the fraudulent scheme. Even when referring specifically to homosexual rights in its official communications, the group was very careful with its selection of words, describing them as "the legitimate rights and interests of homosexuals" (同性恋者合法权益 *tongxinglianzhe hefa quanyi*). The term *hefa quanyi* literally means "lawful rights," with the modifier *hefa* (lawful, legal) emphasizing that the rights in questions are "[in compliance] with the law, being of benefit or at least not being detrimental to society, thus being encouraged, allowed and protected by the law" (Mannoni 2019, 33–34). This terminology is much more neutral than the contentious 人权 *renquan*, "human rights," and it explicitly underlines compliance with existing laws.

In addition to focusing on tongzhi lawful rights as consumers, members of Quancuhui also relied on a common discursive strategy, skillfully inserting the family into the discussion:

> Most of the institutions that claim to correct homosexuality through treatment, they rely on people's lack of understanding of sexual minorities and discrimination. Many homosexuals and their parents have been deceived, and this has not only caused economic losses, but it has also resulted in many homosexuals, like Xiao Zhen,[3] receiving serious harm to their mental health.

Mentions such as this underlined the potential harm the clinic was causing to the parents of patients, a vulnerable and easily deceived group, by promising false solutions for financial gain.

Everyone involved in Yanzi's case continued emphasizing the family angle, especially as more and more media outlets reported on the story. Tongzhi groups and individuals involved in the efforts to make the case visible promoted a narrative in which Yanzi had been pressured by his parents to undergo conversion therapy and was now fighting the clinic to spare other families from the same ordeal. In a WeChat article Quancuhui published on the eve of the trial, the author reports excerpts of an "interview with Xiao Zhen":

> With the court meeting soon, Xiao Zhen actually told us that he has been under great pressure recently. He has increasingly been feeling that this case is not simply a matter of his personal rights, but it is also very important for tongzhi groups and family members. . . . He expects the court to give a fair judgment, letting the deceivers get what they deserve. This way, parents will

no longer force their homosexual children to accept this inhuman treatment.

This narrative was picked up in both international and domestic news,[4] with articles emphasizing that the clinic's false claims preyed on Chinese traditions and on parents' misunderstandings of homosexuality. The appeal to the experience of family pressure, according to Yangzi, also made the case more relatable for young tongzhi who may have undergone the same experience, and helped tongzhi groups generate more interest in the issue.

As the time for the hearing drew nearer, everyone in the community worked to attract as much media coverage as possible. Tongzhi groups and organizers activated their media contacts and made themselves available for interviews and public statements. On the day of the hearing, the largest tongzhi group in Beijing, the Beijing LGBT Center (北京同志中心 Beijing Tongzhi Zhongxin), staged a public performance in which a volunteer in a nurse outfit pretended to perform an electroshock therapy session on a patient lying on the sidewalk. The media attention and widespread coverage was always a large part of the legal strategy—in fact, the inclusion of Baidu in the lawsuit was strategically planned for the sole purpose of generating media interest. Chert, a program manager at the Beijing LGBT Center who had been involved in the media efforts, explained the organization's reasoning:

> At the time, we announced we were suing two places at the same time. One was the clinic, and the other was Baidu. The browser Baidu, like the Chinese Google. Because if you searched for homosexuality on Baidu, a lot of clinics would pop up on the browser, advertising conversion therapy. And the clinic that was being sued at the time was the number one on that list. So we sued both the clinic and Baidu at the same time. Everyone knows Baidu, and we figured this would help our purpose. . . . We were hoping this would encourage everyone to pay attention to the issue of conversion therapy.

When the final verdict was delivered in December 2014, the strategy paid off with an overwhelmingly positive coverage in international news outlets, who hailed the result as "a rare victory for [China's] fledgling gay rights movement."[5]

While international coverage was correct in identifying the victory as a milestone for local groups, reports often omitted some central details of the case that cast a more moderate light on the final verdict. The court did officially affirm that homosexuality is not a mental illness, but it made no conclusions about the legality of conversion therapy. Moreover, while Yanzi received monetary compensation and a written apology, the judge denied that the actions of the clinic constituted an infringement of Yanzi's personal dignity rights as a tongzhi (Parkin 2018, 1251). In fact, much of the victory hinged on the fact that the clinic's director did not have a valid license to perform hypnosis and electroshock therapy (ibid.). The lawsuit against Baidu was also rejected, although the search engine chose to follow the unofficial recommendation of the court and eliminated the clinic's conversion therapy ads from its search results.

Compared to English-language news articles published in the United States and United Kingdom, domestic coverage of the trial paid much more attention to the details of the verdict, and Chinese-language reports made no mention of tongzhi rights. For example, the state-funded (but relatively outspoken) online news site *The Paper* (澎湃 Pengpai News) reported that Yanzi's lawyer in the case followed a strategy focused on three main points: the fact that homosexuality is no longer included in the list of mental illnesses, the fact that the Xinyu Piaoxiang Clinic was only qualified to offer psychological counseling (not psychotherapy), and the fact that the director of the clinic had forged his license.[6] The *Beijing Youth Daily*, the official newspaper of the Communist Youth League Committee in Beijing, also covered the case and, much to the delight of tongzhi groups, reported that homosexuality has been depathologized in China since 2001. At the same time, the article stated that Yanzi's claims regarding the violation of his personal rights had been rejected by the court.

Despite the partial victory, the result of the first tongzhi lawsuit was a significant turning point for the movement. As Chert remarked, "a great achievement [of the lawsuit] was that we were able to say . . . we were able to tell the community that we can use these legal methods to protect our rights, and to tell everyone they should pay attention [to tongzhi issues].” The case crystalized legal advocacy as a feasible avenue for expanding tongzhi visibility in the public sphere and led to important developments both transnationally and within the movement.

Conversion Therapy Case: Transnational Outreach and Domestic Impact

When Yanzi and his team formally filed their lawsuit at the beginning of 2014, they had no clear expectations in terms of outcome. As Yanzi explained, the first lawsuit was mostly an experiment to see if tongzhi advocacy through legal channels could be possible. The high levels of media coverage and the favorable verdict opened up new possibilities for tongzhi groups, particularly on the transnational level.

After Yanzi's hearing in July 2014, members of All Out—a global LGBT rights NGO headquartered in New York and London—reached out to Yanzi and started an online petition in cooperation with Quancuhui. The petition, hosted on the All Out website, collected signatures from all over the world in support of victims of conversion therapy in China, and it included an open letter addressed to the director of the World Health Organization (WHO) Margaret Chan. The goal was to get the support of the WHO and to ask Director Chan to publicly condemn conversion therapy as a medical practice. This type of cooperation mirrors what Margaret E. Keck and Kathryn Sikkink (1998) term a “boomerang model” of advocacy—in which domestic grassroots groups in states offering limited opportunities for political engagement develop ties with global organizations that can, in turn, put pressure on international organizations to achieve results. The model has been shown as having limited effect in the context of China, partly because the creation of transnational links has been connected with an increase in state repression (Long 2018) and partly because pressure from international organizations has a little effect on government practices within the country (Hildebrandt 2012). In the case of the 2014 All Out campaign, transnational efforts didn't quite close the boomerang cycle: the petition generated a lot of interest, collecting over ninety thousand signatures in the first five days, but it fell short of prompting a reaction from WHO director Chan. Articles published by tongzhi groups stopped mentioning the campaign after the first week, and the project was abandoned relatively quickly.

When the final verdict was delivered in December 2014, the positive outcome prompted a new series of efforts on a transnational scale—this time, however, they were more covert due to the potential danger for those involved. Tongzhi activists familiar with Yanzi's case started debating whether it would be a good idea to officially elevate the issue of conversion therapy in China to the level of a human rights crisis, presenting it as such to the international community in the context of the 2015 hearing at the United Nations Committee against Torture (CAT). The CAT is a group of ten human rights experts responsible for monitoring the implementation of the United Nations Convention against Torture, a task they accomplish by requiring regular reports by each state that has ratified the convention. In this setting, it is possible for grassroots groups and NGOs to submit "alternate reports" or "shadow reports" that supplement the official state report. Every four years, the CAT responds to these reports (official and alternate) and produces a nonbinding set of recommendations for the state party. For activists, submitting a shadow report involves putting the Chinese state on the spot, an act that carries a high risk of government retaliation for a potentially small payoff (Parkin 2018).

The issue of whether gaining exposure on the international stage was worth the risk of turning the government hostile was fiercely debated among tongzhi activists, and at the end, a few individuals decided to take action. They activated tongzhi-friendly contacts at the United Nations, relied on intermediaries, anonymized their contributions to minimize risks, and submitted an alternate report that included information about numerous documented cases of conversion therapy used to treat nonnormative sexual orientations.[7] The document mentioned Yanzi's lawsuit and cited international media coverage of the issue, presenting the legal victory as "a first step towards illegalizing such a practice." After submitting the document, tongzhi groups could do nothing but wait and see what would happen at the hearing in Geneva in November.

Their efforts paid off during the final round of questions, when one member of the CAT brought up the issue of conversion therapy. When asked about the existence of conversion therapy clinics and about steps

the Chinese government is taking to put an end to the practice, Yang
Jian, a representative of the Ministry of Justice, gave the following answer:

> As to the issue of LGBTI, mentioned by Madam Gaer and
> Madam Mallah. China does not view LGBTI as a mental dis-
> ease or require compulsory treatment for LGBTI people. They
> will not be confined in mental hospitals either. Indeed, LGBTI
> people face some real challenges in terms of social acceptance,
> employment, education, health, and family life. This deserves
> our attention, but this does not fall within the scope of the Con-
> vention.

The answer was interpreted as an important success for tongzhi advocacy, as it marked one of the few times that the Chinese state went on
record in an international setting to acknowledge the existence and the
struggles of the community. The issue of conversion therapy was also
included in the concluding observations produced by the CAT in February 2016, which also explicitly referenced Yanzi's lawsuit:

> While noting that, in December 2014, a Beijing court ordered
> one such clinic to pay compensation for such treatment, the Com-
> mittee regrets the State party's failure to clarify whether such
> practices are prohibited by law, have been investigated and ended,
> and whether the victims have received redress (arts. 10, 12, 14
> and 16).[8]

Online, tongzhi celebrated the achievement—albeit with no reference
to the fact this was a result of tongzhi activism and with no reference
to the shadow report—and widely reported the words of the state representative. Netizens were particularly impressed by the use of the acronym LGBTI, as the inclusion of intersex individuals signaled to many
the official's unexpected awareness of diversity within the tongzhi community. The most positively interpreted signal, however, was the part
of the statement in which the representative acknowledged tongzhi issues as deserving of the attention of the Chinese government. After the
Geneva hearing, Quancuhui published an article on its official We-

Chat account in which the group detailed the interaction and elaborated on the significance of the result:

> The rights and interests of Chinese tongzhi, especially the right to mental health, have received the attention of the international community, and have even been raised as an issue at the UN level, directly requesting the Chinese government to respond. From originally being depicted as "being mentally ill," and not being seen nor mentioned, tongzhi have now become an issue that the government has to face up to, and one on which it will have to express its position. Such an interaction at the international level is an educational opportunity for Chinese officials, as it allows [them] to understand and recognize the importance of tongzhi rights issues (同志权益议题).

Tellingly, the connection of the CAT to the issue of human rights is never explicitly acknowledged, and the term *human rights* (人权 *renquan*) is avoided in favor of "rights and interests" (权益 *quanyi*) throughout the article. In line with a strategy that focuses on specific needs rather than universal rights, tongzhi groups presented the result as a step toward rights for fair medical treatment and mental health. At the same time, the article also shows a keen awareness of the fact that an official statement in front of an international committee offers no guarantee for results in a domestic setting, especially since CAT recommendations are nonbinding. The author of the article recalls critiques made by tongzhi activists during an event on UN-based advocacy—during which members of the community had questioned the utility of achieving visibility in an international setting—and offers a possible way forward:

> If we don't actively take the statement [of the government official] and use it for advocacy, it is just an "official response" at the United Nations. . . . If we want this positive result to matter for visibility in the country, [we need to] use it for advocacy activities, and even shout to the government: "Those things you said last year, how are those being implemented?" Apply for government information disclosure, ask for specific information,

exert the supervisory power of the people, or use [the official statement] to support your future activities: "You see the official from the Ministry of Justice said that homosexuality is not mental illness . . . (etc.)." It can become a useful tool.

While tongzhi groups, particularly those involved in legal advocacy, seem to have taken the recommendation to heart—frequently citing the official state position on tongzhi issues as presented at the CAT hearing and even including the statement as evidence in subsequent lawsuits—the concrete results many had hoped for have not materialized. The Chinese government has to date made no official statement regarding the legality of conversion therapy as a medical practice, and investigations conducted by various tongzhi groups in the years following Yanzi's lawsuit revealed that conversion therapy is still routinely practiced by clinics in numerous cities around China. In a WeChat article published in May 2019, five years after the first lawsuit, Quancuhui shared the disheartening results of a survey they conducted:

> Five years have passed, and the treatment of homosexuality by domestic medical institutions has not stopped. According to a survey conducted by Quancuhui, among 169 randomly surveyed psychological counseling or related medical institutions in 25 provinces, 107 institutions provide conversion therapy, accounting for 63.31% of the total.

Investigations conducted after the trial further showed that one of the many institutions still offering conversion therapy was none other than the Xinyu Piaoxiang Clinic in Chongqing, the defendant in the first lawsuit (Parkin 2018).

Despite the lack of measurable results in the realm of domestic policy, however, Yanzi's lawsuit had a tremendous impact within the tongzhi community by exposing legal advocacy as a feasible venue to engage in conversation with official channels and to garner the attention of the domestic public. In fact, as I continue showing as I move to the second tongzhi lawsuit in China, subsequent legal efforts were strictly directed toward influencing public opinion and less toward rights-focused transnational cooperation and outreach.

Suing a Government Body:
Qiu Bai's Textbook Case

The second *tongzhi* lawsuit to capture the attention of domestic and international media relied on a similar strategy as Yanzi's case. When it first caught the attention of reporters, the "textbook case" was presented as the story of an individual who, faced with a perceived wrong, decided to pursue legal action to find justice. The motivating incident for the second lawsuit started, according to this narrative, in early 2014, when a nineteen-year-old freshman at Sun Yat-Sen University in Guangzhou went to her college library to find information about same-sex attraction. She turned to a 2013 edition of *Consulting Psychology*, a textbook published by the Guangdong Higher Education Publishing House that is widely used in college classrooms. When she reached the section of the text dealing with same-sex behavior, the information she found included a description of homosexuality as a mental disorder and suggestions on potential cures, including aversion and conversion therapy. She was taken aback by the suggestions and looked for other explanations in other textbooks—but the results were the same.

One year after her discovery, she would become known in domestic and international newspapers as Qiu Bai,[9] the plaintiff of the first Chinese tongzhi rights lawsuit moved against a government body. Qiu Bai sued the Ministry of Education on August 14, 2015, initiating a process that would last over two and a half years and lead to three separate lawsuits, hundreds of news reports, and the inclusion of her case in the 2015 list of "China's Top Ten Constitutional Cases" curated by Renmin University's Research Center for Constitutional and Administrative Law. Qiu Bai eventually lost the case, but the exposure received by "the first case of tongzhi education rights" led to some significant domestic results. At the same time, the case also exposed some key dangers and limitations of legal advocacy for individual plaintiffs.

As in Yanzi's case, Qiu Bai sued the Ministry of Education as an individual, and no tongzhi group was formally involved in any of the lawsuits. Unofficially, however, she relied on the help of Quancuhui to put together her legal team and on local student organizations to support her cause, mobilize students on campus, and garner media attention. The support was particularly important for collecting and disseminating evidence about misinformation printed in college textbooks. In August 2014, a few months after Qiu Bai's textbook discovery and six months before she started trying to get courts to accept her case, a tongzhi organization in Guangzhou published an in-depth, 108-page report titled "Investigation and Report on Content Errors and Stigmatizing Descriptions of Homosexuality in College Textbooks." The report analyzed ninety textbooks widely employed in college courses across the PRC and revealed that more than 40 percent clearly identified homosexuality as an illness and less than 30 percent addressed homosexuality according to the *CCMD-3* guidelines.

The group behind the report was Tongcheng, a tongzhi organization founded in Guangzhou in 2006, and the first Chinese NGO specifically focused on tongzhi youth on university campuses. Tongcheng is also known by its English acronym, GLCAC (Gay and Lesbian Campus Association of China), but most tongzhi refer to the group simply as Tongcheng.[10] The literal translation of the characters 同城 *tongcheng* is "same city" or "local," though of course the character *tong* is the same shared by both *tongzhi* and *tongxinglian*, so the name of the group can be seen as a shortened version of 同志城市 *tongzhi chengshi*, or "tongzhi city." The city in question is Guangzhou University City, an area of Guangzhou where most of the higher education institutions are located and the place where the original members of the group were living in 2006. In its early years, Tongcheng took the form of an informal discussion group where participants could openly talk about the experience of being a sexual minority on a university campus. When the founders graduated in 2010, they decided to continue with the activities and the group transitioned from a localized student group to an off-campus NGO. When I met with organizers and volunteers in 2017, Tongcheng had already reached a nationally recognized status as a key NGO dedicated to improving the quality of life of tongzhi youth through education and outreach. They were mostly active in Guangzhou but had established a larger network spanning nine cities in four provinces and had organized multiple teacher training workshops across the country.

During one of our conversations Cork, one of the original founders of Tongcheng, explained to me the motivations behind the switch from community service to something closer to public policy:

> At first we were doing community service at an internal level, but
> then we actually started getting involved in education, and we
> included activities such as going to schools to share our stories,
> or training teachers.

Cork went on to answer the question of why the group moved to education policy:

> We found that the earlier tactics had actually reached a bottle-
> neck. When we were doing discussions and community service,
> students would talk to us about some of the problems they face,
> but these problems are often related to the whole structure. For
> example, someone may say that their teacher in school said that
> homosexuality is a disease, and then perhaps they would say: "I
> have seen it confirmed on a textbook, it says homosexuality is
> a mental illness."

Addressing structural problems through policy advocacy meant, as in
the case of mental health rights advocacy, carefully striking a balance
between a project of change and a trajectory in line with official state
discourse. The textbook report strives to achieve this balance through
a careful articulation of the problem in a way that exposes the mistakes
in the textbooks, while simultaneously praising the progress of scientific knowledge produced in the PRC. While international standards
are mentioned in the report, authors open the document by analyzing
how discussions of homosexuality and scientific debates *within the PRC*
have changed throughout the years. Errors in textbooks are presented
as problematic because they violate domestic standards, as authors note
that "much of the content related to homosexuality in professional textbooks is inconsistent with domestic scientific standards" and "out of
line with domestic professional views."

At the same time, Tongcheng also strived to draw the attention of
the international community. The report was released during a press
conference with a representative from the UNESCO Asia-Pacific office
and the British Consul General in Guangzhou. There are also parts of
the report that engage explicitly with the language of rights—including
one page in which the authors mention human rights:

In November 2006, the International Commission of Jurists adopted the "Yogyakarta Principles," which apply international human rights law to issues related to sexual orientation and gender identity. Item 16 states that "everyone has the right to education and should not be subject to discrimination based on their sexual orientation and gender identity." . . . In May 2011, the Ministry of Education's "Basic Requirements for the Teaching of Mental Health Education to Students in Ordinary Colleges and Universities" also required that mental health education should be carried out for all college students. The right to know and the right to effective information are part of basic human rights.

The mention is inserted in the first section of the general conclusions, in which authors of the report argue that the lack of content related to homosexuality in college textbooks violates the "right to mental health education" for homosexual students. This refers to increased efforts on the part of the Ministry of Education to provide college students with mental health education and in-school psychological counseling. These efforts culminated in the 2011 set of guidelines mentioned in the report, which required schools to strengthen their curricula for mental health–related classes. The reference to the right to information as a human right is thus meant to paint the limited access to information concerning the mental health of the homosexual community as a violation of both domestic guidelines and human rights. This marks the only instance in the whole report of tongzhi rights being presented as universal rather than specific rights, such as the right to education or to mental health.

The report concludes with recommendations directed at six groups that Tongcheng invites to act in defense of young tongzhi on college campuses: schools and administrators, the education sector, teachers, tongzhi students, NGOs, and scholars. Many of the recommendations advocate for cooperation between tongzhi groups and other actors—for example, teachers are invited to incorporate lectures by members of the tongzhi community in their course plans. When talking about Tongcheng's goals and strategies, Cork explained that cooperation is one of the group's guiding principles—and elaborated on the difficulty of making that explicit while at the same time engaging in policy advocacy:

> This may not be obvious at first, but I think it is possible to promote policy change and cooperation at the same time, in the context of Chinese society. Activities related to public policy are actually considered to be very radical, very sensitive. They are not quite in line with the philosophy we are educated with—because our educational philosophy is that we must be calm and gentle, we must not criticize, we should not go to court and we should not go to the streets.

He further contextualized his remarks by explaining that members of the tongzhi community often express worry at the thought of policy advocacy as a strategy that might be read as oppositional to the government. Instead, he said the work of Tongcheng saw it as precisely the opposite by pointing out that "we need to establish a dialogue. . . . I feel that advocating, or saying that we want to promote change, it is not a matter of standing on the opposite side, it is not a matter of opposing [the government]."

While visibility through research and the production of reports such as the textbook investigation could be interpreted as a way to establish a dialogue, involvement in a lawsuit against the Ministry of Education clearly could not. Therefore, Tongcheng supported the case, but the group did not get publicly involved. The report was sometimes mentioned in relation to Qiu Bai's lawsuit—usually in Chinese-language editions of overseas newspapers[11]—but Tongcheng and the work of the group were seldom mentioned in publications covering the case. In media coverage, the "first tongzhi education rights lawsuit" remained the story of an individual, a framing that protected the groups involved but also ended up exposing Qiu Bai in ways that groups had not predicted.

Visibility and Exposure

Qiu Bai's long involvement in the textbook case began in March 2015, months before she sued the Ministry of Education. At the beginning, she had no intention of suing a government body and her legal efforts focused on the local level. On March 19, she submitted a report letter cosigned with ten other Sun Yat-Sen University students to the Guangdong Provincial Department of Education but received no reply. In May, she attempted to sue the Guangdong Higher Education Publishing House—responsible for publishing the *Consulting Psychology* textbook—but the court rejected the case. At that point, Qiu Bai wrote a letter to the Ministry of Education, asking it to publicly disclose the regulatory measures for the use of teaching materials. Access to the information was her right under the Open Government Information (OGI) Regulations, which protects the freedom of information of Chinese citizens. After receiving no reply from the ministry for three months—the maximum time state bodies are allowed to respond to an information disclosure request—Qiu Bai filed the lawsuit that would bring her case into the spotlight, suing the Ministry of Education on the grounds of administrative inaction.

While everyone was prepared for the case to be high profile, the swift reaction of Sun Yat-Sen University caught Qiu Bai by surprise. Days after the Beijing Intermediate People's Court accepted her case, the university asked Qiu Bai to drop all charges and a school counselor revealed to her parents without her consent that she was a lesbian. Qiu Bai disappeared from social media, leading to widespread online anxiety and speculations of what might have happened to her. On August 26, she resurfaced on her public WeChat account with a tearful message in which she detailed her struggles:

My dear friends, I have disappeared for a few days and made everyone worry. In the past few days, I have deliberately kept my phone off, I just wanted to spend some quiet time with my family. All is still good, but I am a little tired and weak. Tired, tired of coping with school, family, and everyone else. Powerless, because the damage caused by all this cannot be repaired. In just one week, I ended up in an unescapable trap.

The message continues with more details of the meeting with the counselor that her parents were asked to attend as well as the subsequent conversations at home. Qiu Bai explains the difficulty of making her parents understand, stating that "the three characters of *tongxinglian* are too far removed from them. Why don't I want to live a happy life with my parents?" She further anticipates critiques from readers, revealing that she had known being outed as a lesbian was a potential consequence of the lawsuit. She explains she could not muster the courage to come out during a previous visit home.

The intense pressure experienced by Qiu Bai put tongzhi groups in a difficult position—while they had a vested interest in promoting the lawsuit to maximize the visibility of the community, they were also faced with the limitations and dangers of media exposure. While reflecting on these past events in 2017, Cork saw the focus on individual plaintiffs as an even bigger problem, one calling into question the effectiveness of legal advocacy as a strategy for broader change:

> So the media will publish some reports . . . , but these reports are case-by-case, so for example in the media reports, you will see that the articles about Qiu Bai are all talking about her. Her personal story, asking her why she wants to do this, what she did . . . but they may not talk too much about discrimination in the school and in the educational realm. . . . If you just talk about a case, about a single personal story, it's difficult to go deeper, and to talk about problems encountered by the whole community at school.

Cork's frustration is understandable in the context of the textbook case, especially because the final verdict made it painfully clear that media exposure was the only conceivable result of the two-year-long process. After the initial lawsuit was accepted, Qiu Bai was invited to a November pretrial meeting with representatives from the Ministry of Education, where she was convinced to withdraw the lawsuit in exchange for a guarantee that the ministry would promptly address a written complaint on the textbook issue through its supervisory mechanism. Qiu Bai and more than eighty other students from universities around the PRC prepared and sent their complaints as requested but received no response. This prompted a second lawsuit that Qiu Bai filed in April 2016, which was rejected by the court. In June of the same year, she filed a third lawsuit in which she made the case that as a university student, she had a direct stake in the issue of textbook content. She submitted Yanzi's case verdict, the statement of the government official at the CAT, and copies of the *CCMD-3* as evidence that homosexuality is not an illness and requested a complete recall of textbooks containing wrong definitions of homosexuality. While the court accepted the case, it also concluded that Qiu Bai did not have a legal stake in the matter, as "her 'rights to bodily integrity, health, property, and education' were not directly or uniquely involved" (Parkin 2018). She appealed the decision, but after a few months of back and forth, the Beijing High Court made a final judgment against Qiu Bai on March 2, 2017, marking the official end of her lawsuit.

Textbook Case: Domestic Impact

Despite the legal defeat, Qiu Bai's case had important domestic repercussions—both in terms of tongzhi strategies for change and for wording changes in some textbooks. Strategically speaking, Yanzi saw the second lawsuit as a step forward in terms of grassroots mobilization tactics:

> The 2015 case against the Ministry of Education, it was based on the previous one. We perfected our communication strategy . . . and we made good progress in community mobilization. For the conversion therapy case there was no special organization, but in the case of the Ministry of Education we mobilized a large number of student groups.

Efforts to support the plaintiff were indeed coordinated more closely during the lawsuit, especially after groups saw the extreme pressure and public scrutiny faced by Qiu Bai. Groups encouraged members of the community to send messages of support, and organizations like Tongcheng helped coordinate the submission of letters of complaint to the ministry in 2015. As a way to further raise interest in the issue, *tongzhi* were also invited to participate directly in the strategic decision-making process. Following the suggestion of supportive tongzhi groups, in May 2016—after her second lawsuit was rejected—Qiu Bai started a poll on her WeChat account asking users for help in deciding whether to appeal to the Beijing High Court or to apply for administrative reconsideration from the Ministry of Education.

Mobilizing efforts continued after the lawsuit was lost, and eventually led to some of the most significant results for tongzhi on university campuses. Qiu Bai and other students, through the coordinating efforts of Tongcheng, contacted publishers all over the PRC asking them to revise the content of their textbooks. Some of the publishers, including influential education publishing houses such as Renmin University Press, responded positively and promised to update the content.[12] At least in one case, this concretized in a revised edition of a textbook, *Marriage and Inheritance Law*, deleting reference to homosexuality being "against the laws of nature" and changing the sentence "marriage must be between a man and a woman" to "marriage is usually between a man and a woman."[13] Moreover, shortly after the end of the lawsuit Beijing Normal University Press published a controversial sex education textbook for elementary schools that was released for use in thirteen migrant schools in the outskirts of the city and caused great uproar for the explicit nature of the content—which covered not only reproduction but also consent, relationship dynamics, and same-sex attraction.[14] While there seems to be no connection between the textbook lawsuit and the migrant schools' textbook controversy, tongzhi organizers saw it as a sign that presses were paying attention and responding positively.

For Tongcheng, the lawsuit had somewhat mixed results. Even though the group tried to avoid being officially connected to Qiu Bai's legal battle, members of the organization admitted that the media exposure and visibility during the case had made their work increasingly difficult. When we met in 2017, the group was having difficulties organizing any events within college campuses and had given up trying to suggest elective courses on sexuality—at least for the time being. Members of the group were struggling to keep their office space, as their work had attracted too much attention, and they were receiving not-too-subtle hints that they were not welcome there (for example, the organization had recently had water and electricity cut off without explanation). At the time of this writing, Tongcheng's primary WeChat account has been indefinitely blocked and its past articles deleted, though the group is still active on Weibo and on a secondary WeChat account.

While Tongcheng seems to have retreated from the legal spotlight, the organization's efforts have continued and increased on other fronts, such as lobbying academic publishers and training primary and secondary school teachers around the PRC. Training activities in particular have been widely successful and have attracted hundreds of teachers from institutions all over the country. The most effective selling point for these trainings is the idea of inclusive sex and gender education as a strategy to prevent gender violence and bullying—a topic of particular interest for institutions all over China, especially since the Ministry of Education has officially addressed school bullying as a key problem that institutions should work to address.[15] Given the context, the anti-bullying/sex education campaign and trainings seems to fully align with Cork's vision of promoting change while not opposing the government. The success of the trainings and educational activities also speaks to a key aspect of tongzhi policy advocacy, one that relies on the visibility of court cases to promote research and training of professionals on a domestic scale.

Training, Education, and Transnational Negotiations

Since the first two tongzhi lawsuits, legal advocacy in the PRC has emerged as a difficult but expanding arena for political engagement. In the five years between 2014 and 2019, tongzhi plaintiffs have registered multiple legal victories: in 2015, film director Fan Popo filed and won a lawsuit against the State Administration of Press, Publication, Radio, Film and Television (SAPPRFT) for the removal of his movie *Mama Rainbow* from a popular website; in 2016, a tongzhi who goes by the name of Yu Hu filed a lawsuit, won in 2017, against a conversion therapy clinic in Zhumadian where he was forcibly kept for nineteen days, subjected to verbal and physical abuse, and forced to undergo medical treatment for "sexual preference disorder"; in the same year, a transgender man known as Mr. C filed the first transgender employment lawsuit, won in 2018, after being fired from work for wearing masculine clothes despite a female gender marker on his employment ID.

While each of these cases—hailed as examples of victories for LGBT rights in China by international media[16]—represents a significant achievement for the individuals and groups involved, the final verdicts invariably highlight how difficult it is for groups to obtain results that would hold traction for policy change. Yu Hu's victory was based on the clinic's infringement of his personal freedom rather than on the treatment of his sexual orientation, and since the clinic argued that Yu Hu was being treated for an anxiety disorder, the judge made no comment on the legality of conversion therapy or on the definition of homosexuality as a mental illness. Fan Popo won the case because the SAPPFRT argued that it had not issued any documents asking for the film to be taken down, and the judge agreed with that statement (notably, the film was not restored after the verdict). In Mr. C's final verdict, the judge ruled that he was unjustly fired but found insufficient evidence to qualify the case as a gender discrimination case.

While lawsuits typically make small progress on the rights and policy front, an understanding of court cases solely as legal battles for tongzhi rights misses the point of legal advocacy as a pathway to social and cultural—if not legal—change. Yanzi and other tongzhi involved in this kind of advocacy know perfectly well that winning a lawsuit has little bearing on tongzhi rights at the national level. Rather, Yanzi saw each case as a step forward toward tongzhi positive visibility and support in the public sphere:

> [Changing policies] at the national level requires the National People's Congress (NPC). . . . But for now, there is no discussion [of tongzhi issues] in the NPC. The discussion has not yet begun, so the road is quite long. . . . To get them to discuss, I think first we need to change public opinion, which means getting everyone to discuss, getting everyone to be supportive. If we force the relevant people to pay attention, then they have to discuss, so now our strategy is like this. We use a case-by-case strategy to get the public to discuss, and of course, the process is also an educational process.

Yanzi's vision for change resonates closely with the "bottom-up" model proposed by PFLAG's Bear Baba, which I discussed in Chapter 2. While Bear Baba was mostly referring to the process of education of parents, however, groups leaning toward public advocacy have set their sights on different targets: lawyers, educators, and medical professionals who can be made into allies of the tongzhi community and either help groups advocate for change or help the tongzhi community by becoming part of a network of professional allies. The teacher antibullying training organized by Tongcheng is an example of such efforts, and groups around the country are organizing regular conference-like meetings for interested professionals. While in the field, I attended discussions organized by the Beijing lala organization Tongyu in which lawyers discussed the details of Mr. C's legal strategy, and panels in which counselors and psychologists were exposed to debates on gender identity and sexual orientation. Chert, the program manager at the Beijing LGBT Center, directly connected legal advocacy to a need for educating medical professionals:

> Most of the counselors, psychologists and counselors, don't know about gender diversity, which is why they ultimately choose to do conversion therapy. . . . We have done a survey study; we visited more than one thousand psychologist and found that less than 2 percent of them had some knowledge related to gender diversity. So it is very rare. The vast majority of their knowledge comes from the media, or from the news, or from what friends around them say about the LGBT community. . . . So that's why we are doing legal advocacy, and why we are doing these trainings.

This understanding of the potential benefits of legal action resonated with most tongzhi familiar with the court cases. Across the board, most organizers—and even people involved in the lawsuits—prioritized visibility in domestic media as the ideal outcome, as tongzhi presence in the public sphere opened up venues for engaging potential allies. Yanzi characterized it as a trial-and-error process through which groups can carve out new spaces for engagement: "We first cause discussion, and then we rely on the momentum. . . . If we poke here, something moves, so you need to keep poking, you must keep pushing."

Although training and education is directed to professionals in the PRC, educational events and conferences represent opportunities for local groups to engage with transnational LGBT activists and international NGOs (INGOs). On this front, the tongzhi community remains ambivalent—after Yanzi's case, members of Quancuhui have dedicated most of their efforts to domestic cases without much involvement with the international community. Other groups, such as Tongyu and the Beijing LGBT Center, have historically been more involved with transnational organizations and rely on collaborations with INGOs and supranational institutions such as the United Nations to gain international exposure and funding for their training and research activities.[17] Working with INGOs forces these organizations to deal with the uncomfortable tension emerging from the difficult reconciliation of a human rights framework with the political context of the PRC, where—as the careful avoidance of human rights language during court cases shows—human rights are too politically sensitive to be useful. During one of my conversations with Tilia, a researcher at Tongyu who was trying to implement a training program based on the UN Sexual Orientation and Gender Identity (SOGI) framework, she expressed frustration at some of the difficulties of working within a universal human rights framework imposed from INGOs:

> The traditional way to do human rights in the Western world is naming and shaming. It's not going to work here in this context. . . . It's not about doing human rights. It's about humans and their rights. Personally, I don't see eye to eye with maybe the most popular INGOs. I understand they are good people with very good intentions, but I don't see in this context how going against the government, how confronting the government, will bring positive change in the short run. That's my idea. I don't think trying to seek a constructive way to have a dialogue with the government and actually to push forward policy change and improvement on the ground is anything bad or weak or giving in to the government.

The idea of moving from "human rights" to "humans and their rights" mirrors the careful avoidance of renquan (human rights) in favor of quanyi (rights and interests) I have discussed earlier in this chapter.[18] This subtle linguistic shift allows organizers to carefully balance INGO rights-focused rhetoric without ignoring central concerns connected to the political environment in the PRC. Along similar lines, other tongzhi and lala involved in transnational negotiations spoke of the necessity of switching between different discursive approaches when dealing with the international community vis-à-vis promoting rights domestically.

Hyacinth, another researcher at Tongyu who had been involved in activities through the Chinese Lala Alliance (华人拉拉联盟 *huaren lala lianmeng*), a transnational activist alliance between the PRC, Taiwan, and Hong Kong, explained that switching between the two discourses entailed a reframing of rights as protection from violence:

> Human rights . . . it is too sensitive in China. Actually, internationally we do a lot of advocacy within the human rights framework, but in China, we do it in a different perspective; for example, when we want to promote women's rights, children's rights, you do it in a way that . . . you know, you consider them as vulnerable groups, and we need to protect them, in a social protection kind of way. So this is the more acceptable way of promoting rights for minority groups. And this seems to work for LGBT groups right now. When you say "we suffer from violence and discrimination, and this isn't right," you know, and "we should have equal benefits as other people," that is OK. But if you say "we demand human rights," that is not OK.

Hyacinth's strategy of bridging a universal language of rights with a "more acceptable" language of need was a common rhetorical move for policy advocates in the PRC. For activists dealing with transnational organizations, reconciling different approaches to rights advocacy thus takes the form of a careful balancing act, characterized by discursive adjustments and careful linguistic choices—such as reliance on a rhetoric of discrimination rather than human rights. Another key strategy involved discursive work not dissimilar to the alignment with state discourses I discuss in Chapter 3. Nettle, a tongzhi who at the time of our interview was working as a program officer for a regional LGBT program sponsored by the United Nations, described it as a delicate rhetorical dance:

> We try to frame our work not so much as rights based, though it is of course. But we understand the sensitivity, we don't want

to be confrontational. . . . So we find ways. We try to align our discourse with theirs in some way, even though we cannot get a 100% match. But we try to think from [the government's] perspective and to speak their language a little bit.

All these examples show that this discursive bridging is possible, but it risks putting a strain on local organizers. As Tilia's frustration shows, local activists are often the ones who end up caught between the need to maintain a relationship with international donors and the political necessity to avoid being openly confrontational toward the government. As other scholars have documented, divergence on approaches and oppositional attitudes—particularly when it comes to "naming and shaming" the government—is causing significant strain between local NGOs and international or internationally funded organizations (Zhou 2018). As Xi Jinping's ideological battle against Western influences on public opinion intensifies (S. Zhao 2016), maintaining this balance becomes ever more difficult for groups, and some transnational alliances have been forced to dissolve in recent years—particularly following the implementation of the 2017 NGO law that limits and regulates INGO activities in the PRC.[19]

Legal Advocacy, Alliances, and the Challenge of Visibility

This chapter presents legal advocacy as a relatively recent, growing strategy for tongzhi groups to gain public visibility and push for social change. Legal advocacy remains a difficult venue to pursue change: results are uncertain and often only partial, and individual plaintiffs must be fully prepared to sustain intense public scrutiny and exposure. As a strategy, it forces groups and individual tongzhi to face the dilemma of visibility, identified as an explicit goal but also as a major risk. In a recent article, Ian Liujia Tian (2019) calls for an understanding of visibility in the context of tongzhi activism that goes beyond a simple binary of being seen or invisible and suggests that most queer organizing in China strives to remain unseen by the state but visible to other tongzhi organizers. The case studies analyzed in this chapter support the need for a more nuanced understanding of visibility but also suggest that groups are not avoiding the eye of the state—rather, they are carefully trying to achieve a particular kind of lawful visibility that relies on positive representation in the public sphere and on the strategic use of existing legislation and legislative language.

This strategy for visibility can also be read through the lens of what Sophia Woodman (2015) calls "segmented publics," a term she uses to expose the institutional dimension and the rules governing public expression in the Chinese public sphere. By strategically relying on media coverage of the cases, the tongzhi organizations considered in this chapter push the boundaries separating legal and public discourse, "turning a court into a public sphere" (ibid., 105). The exposure that results from this kind of tactic has the potential to influence public opinion and lead to incremental social change, but it can also come at a high price as individuals and organizations find themselves placed under the spotlight. Despite these difficulties, recent legal victories and encouraging developments are contributing to a growing appeal of tongzhi lawsuits among members of the community.

While court cases force tongzhi to engage with the politically contentious language of rights, I show that groups carefully and selectively rely on rights language that avoids the universal terminology of human rights in favor of that of specific, "lawful rights" that presents tongzhi demands as those of ordinary citizens, consumers, and medical patients. I argue that although foreign media and global LGBT organizations tend to understand these lawsuits as confrontational, rights-based advocacy, tongzhi organizers see court cases as a venue to impact public opinion and initiate a dialogue with potential allies—particularly local medical professionals, lawyers, and educators.

Finally, I expose some of the limits and difficulties of transnational collaboration and engagement on the global arena. Although lawsuits that gain international exposure lead to possibilities to work with INGOs and supranational organizations to put pressure on the Chinese government, these efforts entail high risks for potentially minimal payoffs—as scholars and tongzhi activists themselves have pointed out, there is often a marked difference between what the government says in international settings and the policies that end up implemented in the PRC (Piccone 2018). And while collaboration with INGOs is by no means absent, it requires tongzhi organizers to develop discursive strategies that can bridge the gap between approaches based on universal human rights—championed by INGOs—and approaches that are more mindful of the discursive limitations within the political environment of the PRC under Xi Jinping's rule.

Conclusion

A few minutes before 7:00 P.M. on April 13, 2018, the microblogging platform Sina Weibo posted a message on its main page, announcing an upcoming three-month cleanup action with the goal of "creating a sunny and harmonious community environment." The post identified as main target of the action online comics and short videos related to pornography, graphic violence, and homosexuality. The reaction of the tongzhi community was immediate. Shortly after the announcement was made public, a Weibo user going by the handle 竹顶针 Zhudingzhen wrote a short post, stating, "I am gay. What about you?" (我是同性恋。你呢? *Wo shi tongxinglian. Ni ne?*). The post quickly went viral, attracting 14,034 retweets, 4,281 comments, and 23,472 likes within twelve hours (Liao 2019). Tongzhi groups and individual users started flooding Weibo with posts starting with the hashtag #woshitongxinglian (#Iamgay), and the Weibo page connected to the hashtag started attracting increasing amounts of online traffic—reaching over sixty million reads and over sixty thousand tweets and retweets within twelve hours from the original Zhudingzhen post (ibid.).

On April 14, many tongzhi groups published official responses on their WeChat accounts. Many listed official statements about homosexuality as evidence of Weibo's misguided worldview—including the

2001 *CCMD-3*, the 2014 court deliberation regarding Yanzi's conversion therapy case, and the statement made by the Ministry of Justice representative during the 2015 CAT hearing. Quancuhui questioned the legal basis for the ban and mocked Sina Weibo by relying on some of Xi Jinping's favorite language, stating: "[Weibo says that the ban] is inconsistent with the promotion of a 'harmonious community environment,' but perhaps they forgot that the concept of harmonious development refers to 'democracy, the rule of law, fairness, and justice.'"[1] The affiliated lawyer group Rainbow Lawyers posted suggestions on how to file a consumer complaint on the grounds of Weibo's violation of the Consumer Protection Law. And PFLAG drafted an open letter that was sent to the headquarters of Sina Weibo in Beijing, in which the group emphasized the potential disharmonious outcome of the cleanup, shifting the focus on the negative consequences the banning of homosexual content would have on the parents of tongzhi:

> We believe that an inclusive and pluralistic society is conducive to social stability and harmony. Weibo's wrong approach to homosexual content is an act of open discrimination against 42–70 million homosexuals, which makes 84–140 million parents of homosexuals feel sad, distressed, and hurt.

The letter concludes with a quote from *The Communist Manifesto*, reminding Sina Weibo that "the free development of each is the condition of the free development of all." The inclusion of the quote can be read as strategic: Xi Jinping has been vocally promoting a return to Marxism since 2013, when during a speech he identified the abandonment of Marxism as one of the three "confidence crisis" his administration was working to solve.

Encouraged by tongzhi groups all over the country, individual Weibo users continued posting on the website #woshitongxinglian messages. Tongzhi shared their coming out stories, heterosexual allies voiced their support, and parents of tongzhi posted their disappointment in the new online regulations.[2] The online campaign led to a significant payoff. Less than forty-eight hours after the initial Weibo post, tongzhi woke up on April 15 to an unexpected surprise that sent waves of excitement throughout the community: the Chinese edition of the *People's Daily*, the largest newspaper group and the official newspaper of the Central Committee of the Communist Party of China, published a commentary piece on its official WeChat account titled "Different Fireworks Still Sparkle" in which the author explicitly addressed the topic of homosexuality.[3] The focus of the article was actually the Beijing University Press sex education textbook I mention in Chapter 4, but a few sentences toward the end of the article appeared to clearly address the Weibo controversy:

> The mingling of good and bad content on the internet is concerning, but [regulators] need to be careful when handling content, and they should avoid rushing decision and making mistakes by confusing good and bad content. Comparing homosexual content to pornography and graphic violence, and treating homosexuality as an abnormal relationship similar to sexual assault or sexual violence, will inevitably lead to public anxiety.

On April 16, Weibo published a revised version of the announcement. It contained no mention of homosexuality.

Fools and Mountains: The Tongzhi Project of Change

In the midst of the celebrations for the reversal of the Weibo ban on homosexual content, Ah Qiang published an article in which he reflected on the significance of the work of tongzhi groups in the PRC. He wrote: "Few people are willing to follow the spirit of 愚公移山 *yu gong yi shan* [literally "Mr. Fool moves the mountain"]. I also went through a period in which I felt that this was stupid. . . . In the past two years, I have become particularly convinced that the spirit of yu gong yi shan can bring about change." The four characters he mentions are an idiomatic expression referring to the story of old man Yu, who lived in a house in front of two large mountains. The mountains blocked the way and forced members of the Yu's household to walk many miles to go out, so old man Yu decided to remove them by digging away some of the earth a bit at a time and dumping it into the sea. As he began his work, people who saw him mocked his useless efforts, pointing out he would be dead long before he could remove the mountain. Smiling, old Yu replied: "If I die, there will be my sons. And my sons will have grandsons and they will have sons of their own. There will be no end, and the mountain does not grow. One day, it will all be gone." Yu gong yi shan is a story of persistence even when there seems to be little immediate payoff. It teaches that small actions can eventually move mountains.

This study documents tongzhi groups' efforts to challenge and erode existing barriers to tongzhi visibility in the PRC. I argue that understanding these efforts through the lens of contentious, policy-oriented, rights-based political engagement would put us in the position of the people making fun of old man Yu. With no policy gains and no political power, we would say mockingly, What change is there to discuss? And yet the outpouring of support following the Weibo announcement points to a different story, one that perhaps opens the door to a different understanding of change and illuminates a need to consider the existence of different pathways to change.

The analogy of old man Yu and his mountain, however tempting, is of course limited and inevitably erases some of the nuances characterizing the social and political positionality of tongzhi groups and individuals. The mountains tongzhi are trying to remove can—and do—grow, shift, and react to the daily work of groups. While social visibility and support for the community has grown, spaces for political engagement have shrunk in parallel to Xi's administration's growing wariness and hostility toward civil society organizations. Under these conditions, it would make sense to direct our analytical focus to groups' survival strategies rather than change (Franceschini and Nesossi 2018; Spires 2011; Yuen 2015). This book has strived to point to a different path for social scientific inquiry, by focusing on tongzhi groups that—while clearly keeping organizational survival on their mind—pursue a project of change that centers on influencing domestic public opinion and on carving out increasingly large discursive spaces where tongzhi voices can be heard.

By looking at the puzzle of tongzhi strategies for social change in a context where protest and contention is not possible, I have argued for a focus on the linguistic, rhetorical, and discursive tactics that groups adopt and continuously improve on. Tongzhi groups' understanding of cultural change as a prerequisite for political inclusion exposes the centrality of linguistic practices as instrumental elements through which organizations engage in conversation with authorities and with the broader public. And in a political environment where the rules of the game can change drastically and without warning from one day to the next, that discursive adaptability and the capacity to align groups' goals to those of the central government are vital strategic assets for tongzhi organizers.

This book explores how under certain circumstances, it is a purposeful downplaying of tongzhi groups' political work that opens up avenues for political engagement. This was the case for PFLAG, whose success and visibility is connected to their strategy of emphasizing alignment with tradition—particularly through discourses of family belonging and the language of harmony—in order to allow tradition to incorporate change. In other cases, such as those of groups and individuals involved in legal advocacy, achieving visibility in the public sphere meant drawing a distinction between the language of universal human rights and the language of specific rights such as medical or education rights. For groups focusing on research and education efforts, visibility and the possibility to engage in such efforts relied on a presentation of their work as a socially useful service. And for groups treading on a path of transnational cooperation with INGOs, pushing for change meant carefully balancing a language of global rights and activism with the limits imposed by the local political environment.

The arguments presented in this book owe much to social movement theory, transnational sociology, and interdisciplinary work focused specifically on queer China and Asia. Throughout my analysis, I have strived to bring these multiple areas of inquiry in communication with one another. I have endeavored to call into question the overwhelming reliance of social movement literature on models that focus on confrontational tactics, protest, and rights-based strategies as a prerequisite for cultural and political change, suggesting instead that we cross disciplinary boundaries to incorporate models for political engagement that look beyond Western democracies. Contributions from the field of China studies on "nonconfrontational activism" (Wang 2019) have been particularly central to my efforts. By addressing and analyzing linguistic processes and discursive strategies, this book has laid the foundations for an alternative framework that questions and offsets this Western-centric focus, proposing a mechanism for change that is based on discursive engagement, dialogical negotiations, and strategic avoidance of universal rights discourse. This framework simultaneously speaks to literature broadly concerned with the cultural dimensions of political organizing (for some recent examples see Polletta 2012; Polletta and Jasper 2019; Van Dyke and Taylor 2018) and to literature focused on civil society and political mobilization in the specific context of China (see, for example, Hildebrandt 2013; Ho and Edmonds 2008; Keech-Marx 2008; O'Brien and Li 2006; Teets 2014; Wu 2017).

A central characteristic that sets the tongzhi movement apart from other movements in the PRC lies in the liminal position that nonnormative sexual identities occupy in the political sphere—not quite recognized, not officially prosecuted, not officially supported, and just enough removed from the political spotlight to be able to maneuver between shadows and visibility. It is this positioning in a political gray area, I argue, that reveals pathways to change that are not based on a rhetoric of resistance and confrontation but rather on the cultural and social impact of discourses that emphasize tongzhi cultural belonging and social inclusion. The tongzhi political project that I emphasize in this book is one that consciously avoids oppositional practices, and instead relies on the production of narratives of belonging in order to affect and promote social change. As I discuss in Chapter 2, this strategy is not without risks—including the potential crystallization of a homonormative, "high-quality" sexual citizen whose belonging is partly contingent on practices of self-censorship and policing.

My analytical concern with matters related to tongzhi narratives, language, and discursive practices constitutes an effort to deemphasize scholarly notions of the "West" as either a looming and totalizing entity or as the default comparative/mirror to the "non-West." As I discuss in early chapters, the linguistic history of sexual identity labels and sexual subjectivities in the PRC can only be understood transnationally—as the product of multiple processes of negotiation, adaptation, translation (both cultural and linguistic), and constant and fluid reinvention. I have proposed a focus on language and on the creative use of linguistic and narrative ambiguity as a way to embrace a kind of flexibility that questions static binaries of global/local, modern/traditional, colonial/authentic. The limits of these binaries are exposed, for example, in PFLAG's creative reinterpretation of "tradition" and Quancuhui's deliberate use of a specific language of rights.

The road to deconstruct these dichotomies, so deeply engrained into academic scholarship, is still long. I walk on a path initiated by scholars of transnational identities and political processes (Boellstorff 2005; Grewal and Kaplan 2001; Jackson 2001; Lim 2008; Oswin 2004; Sinnott 2012; Kong 2020), approaching tongzhi organizing in the PRC by prioritizing a transnational lens that decenters the West and questions hegemonic epistemologies in the study of nonnormative sexual identities. By doing so, much like the tongzhi groups whose stories I shared, I have tried to make a small dent in the mountain wall.

Keep Digging: Future Directions for Research

In the concluding chapter of her book on queer kinship and family change in Taiwan, Amy Brainer (2019, 116) reminds us of an inescapable truth of this kind of research, stating that "ethnographic research on queer culture is social history nearly as soon as the ink dries." This feels particularly poignant for a book concerned with the action and strategies of groups that occupy a liminal social space in a political context characterized by instability and shifting norms. In the years following my fieldwork and the writing of this book, I have witnessed a further shrinking of spaces for political organizing and, specifically, for the expression of nonnormative identities. I have participated in panels and scholarly discussions on the status of LGBTQ issues in China and followed closely as President Xi's administration doubled down on censoring and regulating nonnormative forms of masculinity on TV and media sites.[4] And while the discursive strategies I have discussed in this book seem to still serve well the tongzhi groups I followed between 2016 and 2019, I have witnessed organizations struggle in ways that I had not seen them struggle while in the field. Just last month, Yanzi announced that Quancuhui is suspending operations for the foreseeable future, and much of the tongzhi legal advocacy efforts are disappearing from public view. Now more than ever, there is a need for research that explores the way groups negotiate their visions of change vis-à-vis an increasingly hostile political environment.

There is also much that this book has not covered and that I wish I could have covered more extensively in my fieldwork. As I address in the introduction, the political conditions of 2017 China were particularly influential in shaping my research questions and in directing, and to some extent limiting, the focus of my empirical observations. This book deals primarily with tongzhi groups who were consciously espousing nonconfrontational tactics—and that I observed being successful in their goals precisely because of this choice. Future research (if conditions make it safe for the individuals involved) should focus on groups that are less able to fly under the political radar due to their commitment to discourses and forms of political engagement that the Chinese state deems more explicitly political or confrontational—this includes, for example, feminist groups and lala organizations that explicitly mobilize queer theory to push against homonormative constructions of tongzhi (national) belonging.

Furthermore, while the label tongzhi and the groups I followed included a wide variety of sexual and gender identities, the data I collected and the events I attended most often spoke to the experience of the gay, lesbian, and bisexual community—with less focus on transgender individuals (with some exceptions). Since the years of my fieldwork, a number of organizations specifically focused on transgender communities have emerged all over urban centers in the PRC, most often in collaboration with health organizations and activists. Future work should look at these important developments, and I hope some of the findings presented in this book will be useful to understand strategies activists are employing to navigate transnational cooperation.

Lastly, an important limitation of this research is the geographic focus on large urban centers. While it is true that most tongzhi organizing happens in large cities such as Beijing, Shanghai, and Guangzhou, the focus on events and interactions in these three metropolitan areas necessarily excludes the voices of individuals who are geographically removed from these centers and who do not travel there to join activities or events. It is imperative to locate the tongzhi experiences I captured during my field work in this urban context and to resist the temptation to generalize my observations.

I believe that in the context of academic writing, leaving readers with new questions holds more value than giving them answers. I hope I have done a bit of both with this book and that scholars coming after me will continue the work of questioning binaries grounded in unequal patterns of knowledge production. Most importantly, for a book focused on narratives and discursive strategies, I hope I have done justice to the stories my participants entrusted to me, and that I have inspired future researchers to explore linguistic and discursive production as a key element in processes of social change.

Methodological Appendix

This research is based on data collected between 2016 and 2019 through a combination of ethnographic fieldwork, semistructured interviews and conversations, and discourse analysis of a variety of online and offline media, ranging from national and international newspapers to WeChat and Weibo posts, independent magazines, and tongzhi groups' pamphlets and brochures. Each of these sources of data allowed me to access different discursive spaces, practices, and strategies, and by combining them and tracking the interactions and overlap across them, I was able to map the rich discursive environment in which tongzhi groups and individuals exist and work toward change.

The majority of ethnographic and interview data comes from six months of fieldwork I conducted in 2016 and 2017 in some of the major urban centers in the PRC. During a preliminary research phase that lasted from September to December 2016, I had informal meetings and conversations with tongzhi groups and individuals in six cities: Beijing, Nanjing, Shanghai, Hangzhou, Guangzhou, and Xi'an. I contacted groups in those cities through their official WeChat accounts, sometimes asking for permission to participate in events and sometimes scheduling informal in-person meetings with members of various organizations. All conversations during this preliminary phase were exploratory in nature—I did not record them, and the present study includes no data collected during those months. Those early meetings shaped the final project in important ways, as they were crucial to establish a network of potential research participants, build rapport, understand the organizational field, and familiarize myself with the specific discursive practices of the tongzhi community. It was during those initial months that I learned of activities being planned for the following summer—by far the busiest time of the year for tongzhi groups—and it was through tongzhi contacts I met in the preliminary research phase that I was invited to participate in many of them.

Following those first three months in the field, I decided to limit the geographical scope of the project to the three urban centers of Beijing, Shanghai, and Guangzhou. I chose these cities in part for their national, political, and cultural importance and in part because they are the three locations with the highest concentration of tongzhi groups, as well as those in which the largest and most influential organizations have their headquarters.[1] And while most of my interviews and participant observations were conducted in the three urban centers, I do not see my research strictly confined to those geographical spaces. Most of the events I attended were organized by groups who are active across multiple provinces and municipalities and whose activities attracted participants from all over the country. Analyzing these groups' practices, strategies, and conceptualizations of change meant engaging with their work beyond the city in which they were headquartered, and speaking to attendees at various events brought me in contact with tongzhi from many different cities and provinces. That said, my study did capture a predominantly urban experience—the tongzhi I interviewed had often come into contact with groups in the context of events organized in a city where they either studied or worked, and even those whose families lived in smaller towns and rural areas had only become involved in tongzhi activities after moving to an urban area.

Ethnographic Fieldwork

My preliminary work in the field was crucial in terms of identifying and gaining access to key tongzhi organizations to include in my study. I conducted the majority of my participant observations at events organized by some of the largest and most visible groups active in the PRC, namely PFLAG, Tongyu, the Beijing LGBT Center, Tongcheng, and a few lala groups connected to the transnational Chinese Lala Alliance. While I also attended events organized by smaller and less formal groups, they make up a minority of observational data. Although my reliance on events organized by these relatively large organizations active on a national and transnational scale risks erasing diversity and underrepresenting groups working on a regional or local scale, I consider the visibility and meaning-making power of these larger organizations as a signal of their potential to influence the broader community and to significantly shape the discursive field. This was confirmed during my conversations with members of smaller, local groups, who demonstrated clear awareness of the work of the larger groups and who often participated in events that these groups organized.

The summer of 2017 turned out to be a serendipitously appropriate time to conduct participant observation at tongzhi events. As I mention in Chapter 2, the year marked the tenth anniversary of PFLAG's kentanhui, prompting the group to organize a large-scale, multiday celebration on board a cruise ship traveling from Shanghai to Fukuoka (Japan). Thanks to the help of some PFLAG volunteers I had met and befriended in Beijing in 2016, I was able to secure a spot on the cruise ship and thus found myself in what I often describe as an ethnographer's paradise: I was quite literally stuck in the middle of the ocean with eight hundred potential research participants and four days of events and activities happening around the clock. Moreover, the anniversary celebration was an occasion for PFLAG members to reflect on the achievements of the past decade—thus making the notion of change central to many of the cruise events.

Because of the particular setting on a ship, those four days were the most intense among all the time I spent in the field. While official activities ended around 9:00 P.M., informal meetings and discussion continued well into the night, and it was not unusual for young tongzhi to wait for the sunrise while chatting and playing cards on one of the decks. I tried to strike a balance between wanting to participate in as many events as possible and securing enough time to type and organize field notes on my laptop, add memos to interview files, and eventually get some sleep. I tried to alternate nights in which I would participate in late night games and discussions and nights in which I would go to sleep early to then meet mothers exercising on the upper deck in the early hours of the morning. While exhausting, this alternating schedule allowed me to build positive relationships with both young tongzhi and their parents, giving me the opportunity to recruit research participants from both groups.

In addition to PFLAG's kentanhui, I attended a total of twenty-three events and activities organized by tongzhi groups in and around Beijing, Shanghai, and Guangzhou. These varied widely in terms of focus and included workshops, structured discussions, film screenings, expert debates, museum exhibits, and more. Sometimes events would be planned in advance and advertised on WeChat, and sometimes I would hear about them from individuals and be invited to private online conversations where the location of the meeting would be revealed at the last second via text message. Some events were open to the whole community, while others were LBT events open only to individuals who identified as women. Attending events not only helped me develop rapport with members of the community but also allowed me to "capture fluid, shifting conditions . . . [and] to trace developing mobilization patterns in embedded social contexts; identifying key issues, such as the way social actors are framing the stakes of engagement" (Plows 2008, 1524). The vast majority of the weekly meetings I attended left ample space for attendees' active participation, effectively becoming "interactional spaces for critically reflexive discussions" (Balsiger and Lambelet 2014, 147) on topics ranging from identity and coming out to visibility of the community, current and future goals, and group strategies.

With the exclusion of a few film screenings in Shanghai and a few social gatherings organized by the Beijing LGBT Center, I was the only foreigner at most of the events that I attended as a participant-observer. This turned out to be an advantage, as my presence was noticed immediately by event participants, who often approached me, welcomed me, and introduced me to their friends. Whenever the structure of the event allowed it, I contacted organizers in advance to ask if I could briefly introduce myself as a researcher to the audience, a request that was received positively most of the time. I introduced myself speaking Chinese, and identifying myself as "an Italian lala pursuing a PhD at the University of Chicago." This introduction consistently generated a lot of interest in events attendees: my knowledge of Chinese and reliance on lala as an identity label signaled linguistic and cultural competence, as well as my belonging to the community, and my cross-cultural identity as an Italian living in the United States always led to questions and conversations about the status of LGBT individuals in those countries. On two occasions during PFLAG events, I was invited on stage to share my coming out story and to answer questions about parental acceptance in Italy. My introductions were also a primary recruitment method for interviewees, as after identifying myself as a lala researcher, I would invite event attendees interested in taking part in my project to approach me at the end of the event.

Interviews

I relied on interviews as a primary data collection method as much as participant observation. Interviews have always played a key role in social movement research, as they are well-suited for inquiries about individuals' reasons for participation, their understanding of the movement, and the activities of organizations (Blee and Taylor 2002). I initially opted for semistructured, in-depth interviews because of their potential to shed light on processes of change and particularly on the interpretation participants give of such processes (della Porta 2014). As I interviewed participants and organizers, I paid attention both to their experience within the group and to the understanding of the social and political reality of contemporary China that guided participants' involvement in the tongzhi community and movement.

My interview data comes from a pool of 107 individuals, the majority of which (74 percent) identified as members of the tongzhi community. The remaining participants were actively involved in community events as either parents of tongzhi (23 percent) or as teachers who had participated to training workshops offered by tongzhi groups (3 percent). Almost half (44 percent) of the tongzhi I interviewed were involved in group activities as organizers, leaders, or volunteers. All participants were Chinese nationals, and the vast majority of the interviews (92 percent) was conducted in Chinese (Putonghua). I also conducted interviews with two LGBT expats in Beijing and Shanghai, but I decided not to include this data due to the limited involvement of these individuals with local tongzhi groups.

I collected interview data through a combination of fifty-two formal, semistructured in-depth interviews and hundreds of informal, semistructured and unstructured conversations. All formal interviews were audio-recorded and transcribed, while for informal conversations I relied on memory, notes I discretely wrote on my notebook and phone, and voice memos that I recorded immediately after each conversation and later transcribed. While formal interviews had the distinct advantage of allowing me to record the words of my participants, I found informal conversations much more useful and illuminating. It was easier to build rapport with participants without the presence of my audio recorder on the table, and more than once, I found myself talking to individuals I had previously interviewed and finding the informal conversation more natural and helpful. This was particularly evident with mothers and fathers of tongzhi, who were much more inclined to share their experiences and opinions outside the formality of an interview setting. A few parents initially turned down my requests for an interview by explaining that they didn't think their opinions were worthy of being recorded—however, they were more than happy to chat with me over a meal, and they allowed me to use the parts of the conversation I found useful. I also quickly realized conversations with parents were particularly beneficial when more than one parent was present—mothers and fathers would build on each other's stories, debate interpretations of events, and encourage each other to explain things to me when they thought it necessary.

Formal interviews ranged in length from thirty-five minutes to four hours, with an average length of one hour and fifteen minutes. The length of informal conversations varied depending on the situation—sometimes they would only last a few minutes during breaks at various events; sometimes they lasted multiple hours during meals or social events. While I allowed for interviews and conversations to develop organically and move in directions not fully within my control, I also memorized a topic guide covering issues concerning identity and self, involvement with tongzhi groups, changes in the social and political environment of the PRC, the current work and future hopes of tongzhi groups, and the perception of sexual identity movements outside of the PRC. I constantly updated this guide throughout my time in the field, for example adding questions on specific events that had recently happened or incorporating topics that I noticed were being discussed online by members of the community.

All interviews conducted in 2017 were in person. I had one follow-up conversation with Yanzi via audio message in 2019, as I wanted to ask him a few details about past and recent lawsuits. For in-person interviews, I let my participants select the location they preferred, which resulted in a wide array of interview settings. Locations varied from public spaces such as cafes and restaurants to the headquarters of tongzhi organizations, empty office spaces, train stations, participants' private apartments, and parks. I always offered my own accommodations as an option, and on two occasions, I conducted interviews in the apartment I was renting. Many of the interviews with PFLAG's members were conducted aboard the cruise ship—sometimes in my own cabin, other times out on the deck, and often in one of the many sitting areas near the dining hall.

After collecting the first few interviews, I began preliminary coding on the audio files. I coded directly on audio files because I was gathering interview data faster than I could transcribe them, but I found coding and adding memos while listening was an effective method to start identifying thematic and rhetorical patterns. Coding on the audio files also allowed me to mark moments in the interviews where participants revealed identifying information about themselves or mentioned a third party by name. Once I left the field, I edited the audio files to erase this information and sent my interviews to a professional transcription company. After receiving the transcribed text, I initially coded it with the code system developed on the audio files and then refined the system through a second round of coding. I paid particular attention to the semantic context of statements (Blee and Taylor 2002), analyzing participants' use of language as a means of identity construction (Davis 2002; Polletta 2006) and as a tool to define "individual and collective visions, imaginings, hopes, expectations, critiques of the present, and projections of the future" (Blee and Taylor 2002: 95). I added rough translations to the original Chinese text and then provided more sophisticated and faithful translations of the segments that I would include in the book.

For all my coding, I relied on the mixed-methods and qualitative data analysis software MAXQDA—initially relying on MAXQDA12 and then switching to the updated version MAXQDA2018 in December 2017. The software allowed me to link audio files to transcription files and to write and connect multiple levels of memos to codes, files, and single-text sentences within each file. I also imported into the program my notes and the audio recordings I made after each informal conversation, thus building a single library containing data from both interviews and conversations. The ability to link various types of file to each other proved particularly labor-saving for analysis of conversation data, which was often spread across multiple media and most of the time consisted of a combination of notes and memos in multiple languages.

Content Analysis

In addition to ethnographic fieldwork and interviews, I relied on a discursive and content analysis of online materials as a supplemental source of data. While I was in the field, I started saving and importing into my MAXQDA project articles about the events I was attending that groups published on their official WeChat accounts. I considered looking at the discursive and rhetorical repertoires employed by groups in an official capacity a necessary step to understand their strategies for mobilization and their models of change. Social movement scholars have recognized the normalization of identities and the diffusion of contentious terms and discourses as one of the ways organizations have to affect the sociocultural landscape they operate in (Polletta 2006; Polletta and Jasper 2001; Tarrow 2013; Williams 1995). For example, framing theorists have pointed out how the creation of master frames (Snow and Benford 1988, 1992) can crystalize contentious debates by privileging a particular approach to an issue (Oliver and Johnston 2000).

Crystallization, however, suggests a static discursive field. Instead, I relied on media analysis to investigate the dynamic negotiations embedded in the process of meaning construction (Fine 1995; Gamson 1988). To do so, in addition to WeChat publications I saved international and local newspaper articles dealing with tongzhi issues and activities. This allowed me to compare discourses across multiple media and to examine the cultural and symbolic struggle tongzhi organizers engaged in as they defined issues, goals, aspirations, and ideas (Kane 1997; Steinberg 1998; Davis 2002). I could also track the differences between what was said during events and activities and what was reported on public articles prepared by members of the group in charge of them, thus collecting vital information on the discursive strategies on which groups relied to gain visibility in the public sphere.

For events I attended or that happened while I was in the field, I collected online materials in real time—sometimes necessarily so, as some WeChat articles were censored soon after publication—while for events that had happened in the past I had to track down relevant articles by searching the WeChat history of various groups. To track down newspaper articles, I relied on a combination of word searches on search engines such as Google and Baidu and keyword searches on the online pages of specific newspapers as well as reviewing links tongzhi organizers shared with me.[2] While I systematically collected tongzhi groups' WeChat and Weibo publications for a separate research project—building a database in excess of twenty thousand articles—for this study I analyzed only the small subset of those that was relevant to the events I discussed. I coded a total of sixty-two newspaper articles and ninety-five WeChat publications as well as a few research reports independently produced by tongzhi groups.

Last but certainly not least, no methodological discussion on research in contemporary China would be complete without a discussion of the importance of WeChat. The centrality of this social media platform is certainly already emerging from my heavy reliance on it for the collection of articles published by tongzhi groups, but there is much more to this app. WeChat functions are used to coordinate activities, collect donations, and reserve spots at closed-number events.

Tongzhi organization leaders often invited me to large WeChat discussion groups, adding me to the conversation and introducing me to the rest of the group members. These introductions by well-known and respected members of the community were crucial to solidify my standing and to legitimize my presence at events.

Because of the ubiquitous presence of WeChat as a networking tool, my initial plan to avoid getting WeChat profile information from research participants soon proved impractical or sometimes downright impossible. Refusing to exchange WeChat barcodes is a breach in etiquette, and it would have been completely counterproductive to my research. A WeChat group was created for every event and social outing I attended, and tongzhi organizations usually projected the barcode link to the group discussion on a screen at the beginning of each event. Event attendees could then use the group to discuss, connect with one another, and share pertinent links and information. Sometimes group members would contact me or offer to answer any research questions I might have on WeChat, but I always declined their offers and usually proposed an in-person meeting instead. Members of the tongzhi community are aware of the fact that WeChat conversations are fully accessible to Chinese authorities and refrain from saying things that may attract the ire of censors, but given the unpredictability of government reactions and its somewhat contradictory relationship to the tongzhi community, I decided it was not worth it to risk having my informants' thoughts and opinions on the tongzhi movement voiced on the nonencrypted platform.

Notes

Introduction

1. As I explain in more detail in Chapter 1, homosexuality has never been technically criminalized in China. The year 1997 marks the elimination from the Chinese Criminal Code of the "crime of hooliganism," which police often relied on to punish individuals engaging in same-sex behavior.

2. For a list compiled in 2012 and updated intermittently between then and 2016, see Liu Xiaomian, Zhihu question thread "What LGBT organizations are there in China?" November 8, 2012, https://www.zhihu.com/question/2057 8932.

3. CGTN is an English-language news channel of the state-owned China Global Television Network group, and it is part of the Beijing-based state television broadcaster China Central Television (CCTV). It was formerly called CCTV-9, and it is primarily aimed at an overseas, English-speaking audience.

4. Part of the appeal of WeChat lies in the fact that the app condenses most services and functions Chinese users utilize in everyday life into one neat package. Aside from the social platform component, the app is used as a payment platform for taxis, event tickets, hotel reservations, and so on. WeChat barcodes are also increasingly used in advertisement and on business cards.

5. CPC History Publishing and Party Construction Readings Publishing House, "Decision of the Central Committee of the Communist Party of China on Several Major Issues Concerning the Construction of a Socialist Harmo-

nious Society," www.gov.cn, last accessed 4/1/2023, http://www.gov.cn/govweb /gongbao/content/2006/content_453176.htm.

6. The increased level of online scrutiny and censorship was such that Chinese netizens started referring to the practice of having posts censored or taken down as "being harmonized" (被和谐了 *bei hexiele*).

7. A complete translation of Document 9 is available at ChinaFile, "Document 9: A ChinaFile Translation," November 8, 2013, http://www.chinafile .com/document-9-chinafile-translation#start.

Chapter 1

1. As it turns out, the "small municipality" of Puning is home to two million people, half a million more than my hometown of Milan, the second-most-populous city in Italy.

2. Most tongzhi use their internet nicknames as pseudonyms and often choose names of natural elements, animals, and similar. I have changed my informants' pseudonyms but kept the nature connection.

3. Both *tongxinglian* and *tongxing'ai* were translated through Japanese translations of Western sexology texts. The Japanese translation of "sex" into the kanji *sei* became *xing* in Chinese, and *doseiai* was translated as *tongxing'ai*, *tongxing lian'ai*, or *tongxing lian*—all gender-neutral terms meaning "same-sex love" (Kong 2010; Sang 2003). The term that gained the biggest traction, and that is still used today, is *tongxinglian*.

4. Sodomy is understood as nonreproductive sex between two men.

5. In an effort to collect their stories, Creek had started an oral history project in Guangzhou that is still in progress at the time of this writing: 广州老年 男同志口述史

6. The term *tongqi* combines 同 *tong*, the first character of *tongzhi* and *tongxinglian*, with 妻 *qi*, the first character of *qizi*, "wife."

7. The full manifesto is accessible at Utopia, "1996 Chinese Tongzhi Conference Manifesto," accessed June 4, 2019, https://www.utopia-asia.com/tong zhi.htm.

8. Hooliganism—a broadly defined offense designed to encompass all those activities perceived as a danger to the social order—was cut from the Criminal Law as part of a large-scale effort to eliminate blurry and unclear definitions from the criminal code (H. Tanner 2000).

9. "Come out" here is intended as "leave the house to go to gathering," not as "come out of the closet."

10. There is no law that explicitly forbids local civil affairs bureaus to register tongzhi organizations, but officials generally refuse to do so on the grounds of political/social/moral sensibility.

11. The three NOs are 不支持, 不反对, 不提倡 *bu zhichi, bu fandui, bu tichang* and have been variously translated as "no approval, no disapproval, no promotion"; "don't support, don't disapprove, don't promote"; and other similar variants.

12. Data compiled from yearly reports released by the China Internet Network Information Center (CNNIC). For a list of all the available Statistical Surveys on Internet Development in China, see https://www.cnnic.com.cn/IDR/ReportDownloads/. See also reports on The Internet Timeline of China available at https://www.cnnic.com.cn/IDR/hlwfzdsj/.

13. This is the pseudonym she uses within the community, and the one she is most known by. At the time of our interview, she authorized me to refer to her as Xian in my work.

14. The limits of internet accessibility are of course important and contribute to further skewing the development of the community toward well-connected urban areas.

15. Qiu Miaojin was the first woman in Taiwanese literature to publicly come out as lesbian, and her book provided the underground Taiwanese lesbian community with a vocabulary to talk about same-sex attraction and identity. Qiu Miaojin is also considered a lesbian martyr, as she killed herself at the age of twenty-six, one year after publishing her novel. After her death, *Notes of a Crocodile* became a cult novel for Taiwanese lala.

16. I am relying on the English translation included in the journal here.

Chapter 2

1. Blued and LesDo are tongzhi dating apps.

Chapter 3

1. The date, 520, is read as five-two-zero, which in Chinese produces a sound (*wu er ling*) similar to "I love you" (*wo ai ni*).

2. The Bund is a waterfront promenade along the Huangpu River, arguably the most symbolic space in Shanghai. The whole area was a British settlement in the mid-1800s.

3. The main sponsors for the event were Blued, the China-based largest gay social network app in the world; 西瓜旅游 (Pumpkin Travel), a transnational LGBT travel company; and 初恩宝贝, a Shanghai company specialized in IVF and adoptions in the United States.

4. One evening while on board, I was also accosted by a plainclothes policeman who inquired about my presence. He asked whether I was a diplomat or a representative of my country and seemed satisfied with my explanation. Once

I became legible as an Italian student, he closed the conversation fairly quickly and did not ask any more questions for the duration of the trip.

5. Usually translated as "double happiness," 囍 is a ligature made of two 喜 *xi* characters, meaning "happiness."

6. The characters for "he" (他) and "she" (她) are both pronounced *ta* and, therefore, require the same sequence of letters, t + a, when typed on a keyboard. The use of one instead of the other could thus be conceivably seen as a typo.

7. One of the ten couples withdrew from the ceremony at the last second.

8. A *qipao* is a fitted dress with a high mandarin collar, dating back to the Qing dynasty.

9. The *South China Morning Post* is a Hong Kong English-language newspaper owned by Alibaba Group and available throughout the PRC.

10. Liu Mindan, "Shanghai: Parents of Tongzhi Looking for Marriage Matches for their Children at the Matchmaking Corner Removed [from the park]." Zhongguo Qingnian Wang [China Youth Network], 22 May 2017, https://news .china.com/socialgd/10000169/20170522/30552868_all.html.

11. Zhang Yingying, "A Special Wedding on Board," Noon, 10 July 2017, https://www.sohu.com/a/155904956_550958.

Chapter 4

1. See for example Dan Levin, "Chinese Court Sides with Gay Man in 'Conversion' Suit," *New York Times*, December 19, 2014, https://www.nytimes.com /2014/12/20/world/asia/chinese-court-sides-with-gay-man-against-clinic-that -tried-to-convert-him.html; Jonathan Kaiman, "Chinese Court Rules 'Gay Cure' Treatments Illegal," *The Guardian*, December 19, 2014, https://www.theguard ian.com/world/2014/dec/19/chinese-court-gay-straight-conversion-clinic; Robert Foyle Hunwick, "Beijing Court Orders Clinic to Compensate Gay Man for 'Treating' His Sexuality," *The Telegraph*, December 19, 2014, https://www.tele graph.co.uk/news/worldnews/asia/china/11304309/Beijing-court-orders-clinic -to-compensate-gay-man-for-treating-his-sexuality.html.

2. At the time of writing, there have been a total of ten cases involving a sexual minority plaintiff.

3. The pseudonym Yanzi was using in court at the time.

4. See for example Celia Hatton, "China Court Accepts 'Gay Conversion Therapy' Case," BBC News, May 21, 2014, https://www.bbc.com/news/blogs -china-blog-27498288; Bill Powell, "Gay Conversion Therapy Lives On in China," *Newsweek*, September 17, 2014, https://www.newsweek.com/2014/09/26 /chinese-quack-selling-gay-aversion-therapy-sued-victim-270997.html.

5. The line, taken from *The Telegraph*, was cited widely by tongzhi groups on WeChat. The original article can be found at Robert Foyle Hunwick, "Beijing Court Orders Clinic to Compensate Gay Man for 'Treating' His Sexual-

ity," *The Telegraph*, December 19, 2014, https://www.telegraph.co.uk/news/world news/asia/china/11304309/Beijing-court-orders-clinic-to-compensate-gay-man -for-treating-his-sexuality.html.

6. Zhou Chen, "The First 'Gay Conversion' Case Was Heard in Beijing, and the Clinic Was Accused of 'Three Major Crimes,'" *The Paper*, August 2, 2014, https://www.thepaper.cn/newsDetail_forward_1259405.

7. The alternate report is available from the UN Treaty Database: Chinese Human Rights Defenders, *Civil Society Information Submission to the Committee against Torture for the Review of the Fifth Periodic Report of China (CAT/C/CHN/5): Specific Information on the Implementation of the Convention against Torture and Other Cruel, Inhuman or Degrading Treatment or Punishment*, February 9, 2015, https://tbinternet.ohchr.org/_layouts/15/treatybodyexternal/Download.aspx ?symbolno=INT%2fCAT%2fNGO%2fCHN%2f19726&Lang=en.

8. Committee against Torture, "Concluding observations on the fifth peri-odic report of China," 3 February 2016. Full document available at https://tbin ternet.ohchr.org/_layouts/15/treatybodyexternal/Download.aspx?symbolno=CAT %2fC%2fCHN%2fCO%2f5&Lang=en.

9. For this and for all the other cases mentioned in this chapter, I rely on the pseudonyms plaintiffs used in court and by which they were addressed in media reports. Yanzi is the only exception, as he is mentioned under various pseu-donyms (the most common being Xiao Zhen, Yang Teng, and Yanzi Peng) in media coverage of the trial but has since assumed Yanzi as his preferred pseu-donym.

10. Tongcheng is the shortened version of the group's official Chinese name, 同城青少年资源中心 (Tongcheng Qingshaonian Ziyuan Zhongxin, TongCheng Youth Research Center).

11. See, for example, Buckley, "Chinese Gay College Students Speak with Ministry of Education Officials," *New York Times, China*, November 25, 2015, https://cn.nytimes.com/china/20151125/c25chinatextbook/ and BBC News, China, "Chinese Court Accepts Female College Student's Lawsuit against Min-istry of Education for Stigmatizing Homosexuality," June 16, 2016, https://www .bbc.com/zhongwen/simp/china/2016/06/160616_china_textbooks_homo sexuality.

12. Qian Jinghua, "China's Homophobic Textbooks Turn Over a New Leaf," Sixth Tone, April 24, 2017, http://www.sixthtone.com/news/1000050/chinas -homophobic-textbooks-turn-over-new-leaf.

13. Qiu Bai, "Homosexuality is against the laws of nature? The first step of the legal vanguard is to revise homophobic textbooks," Zhihu post, 4 Novem-ber 2017, https://zhuanlan.zhihu.com/p/30733113.

14. Distribution of the book was halted shortly after images started circulat-ing online, as parents felt the images and discussion were too explicit for their children.

15. The Ministry of Education released guidelines against school bullying in 2016 and laid out a comprehensive plan to tackle bullying in primary and secondary schools in December 2017. The plan is available here: Ministry of Education of the People's Republic of China, "Circular of 11 Departments Including the Ministry of Education on Printing and Distributing the 'Strengthening the Comprehensive Treatment Plan for Bullying of Primary and Secondary School Students,'" Jiaozhu [2017] No. 10, November 23, 2017, http://www.moe.gov .cn/srcsite/A11/moe_1789/201712/t20171226_322701.html.

16. See, for example, Lilian Lin, "Chinese Gay Activist Claims Victory in Online Film Censorship Lawsuit," *Wall Street Journal*, December 28, 2015, https://blogs.wsj.com/chinarealtime/2015/12/28/chinese-gay-activist-claims-victory-in-online-film-censorship-lawsuit/; "Gay Chinese man wins legal battle over forced conversion therapy," *BBC News*, July 4, 2017, https://www.bbc.com/news /world-asia-40490946; Benjamin Haas, "Chinese transgender man wins landmark wrongful dismissal case," *The Guardian*, January 3, 2017, https://www .theguardian.com/society/2017/jan/03/transgender-man-in-china-wins-wrongful-dismissal-case.

17. In part, this is connected to the transnational history of these two organization. I detail the history of Tongyu in Chapter 1. The Beijing LGBT Center was created when Tongyu and a few other groups of local and foreign lala and tongzhi decided to rent an apartment and make the space into a tongzhi community center.

18. Tilia was one of the few participants who preferred to be interviewed in English, but her formulation is strikingly close to the distinction between the two words in Chinese.

19. The Chinese Lala Alliance was one of the transnational networks impacted by the law, and the organization was dismantled in early 2018.

Conclusion

1. These four elements, in quotation marks in the original, are a favorite list of President Xi.

2. A message from a PFLAG mother from Shanghai collected over sixty thousand likes, almost ten thousand retweets, and over six thousand comments. In it, she called out Sina Weibo for the damage the website was bringing to China's reputation by stating: "I am the mother of a gay child. My son and I love our country. No matter where we go, we always tell other people we are from China! We are proud of being Chinese! But today I saw Weibo's public announcement. . . ."

3. The title, a reference to a song by bisexual Hong Kong singer, Leslie Cheung, was later changed to the more direct "Homosexuality is not a mental illness."

4. Publicity Department, "Notice of the General Office of the State Administration of Radio and Television on Further Strengthening the Management of Cultural Programs and Their Personnel," Radio and television Office [2021] No. 267, National Radio and Television Administration, September 2, 2021, http://www.nrta.gov.cn/art/2021/9/2/art_113_57756.html.

Methodological Appendix

1. Among many others, Beijing hosts the headquarters of Tongyu, the Beijing LGBT Center, Tongzhi Yi Fanren (all three on different floors of the same building); Guangzhou hosts PFLAG's headquarters, the editorial office of the *Queer Lala Times*, Tongcheng's headquarters, and Quancuhui (which doesn't have a physical office); Shanghai hosts Shanghai Nüai, a large PFLAG branch, and it was the starting point for PFLAG's 2017 cruise.

2. Because groups care deeply about the way their work is represented on mainstream media (especially if it happens to be a state-owned newspaper), organizers and volunteers keep track of articles in which tongzhi activities or groups are mentioned.

References

Altman, Dennis. 1996. "Rupture or Continuity? The Internationalization of Gay Identities." *Social Text* 48 (3): 77–94.

———. 1997. "Global Gaze/Global Gays." *GLQ* 3 (4): 417–36.

Amenta, Edwin, Neal Caren, Elizabeth Chiarello, and Yang Su. 2010. "The Political Consequences of Social Movements." *Annual Review of Sociology* 36 (1): 287–307.

Amenta, Edwin, and Francesca Polletta. 2019. "The Cultural Impacts of Social Movements." *Annual Review of Sociology* 45 (1): 279–99.

Andrews, Kenneth T., and Neal Caren. 2010. "Making the News: Movement Organizations, Media Attention, and the Public Agenda." *American Sociological Review* 75 (6): 841–66.

Armstrong, Elizabeth A. 2002. *Forging Gay Identities: Organizing Sexuality in San Francisco, 1950–1994*. Chicago: University of Chicago Press.

Arthur, Mikaila Mariel Lemonik. 2011. *Student Activism and Curricular Change in Higher Education*. Burlington, VT: Ashgate.

Balsiger, Philip, and Alexandre Lambelet. 2014. "Participant Observation." In *Methodological Practices in Social Movement Research*, edited by Donatella della Porta, 144–72. Oxford: Oxford University Press.

Banaszak, Lee Ann, and Heather L. Ondercin. 2016. "Public Opinion as a Movement Outcome: The Case of the U.S. Women's Movement." *Mobilization* 21 (3): 361–78.

Bao, Hongwei. 2018. *Queer Comrades: Gay Identity and Tongzhi Activism in Postsocialist China*. Copenhagen: NIAS Press.

———. 2020. *Queer China: Lesbian and Gay Literature and Visual Culture under Postsocialism*. New York: Routledge.

Biddulph, Sarah. 2015. *The Stability Imperative: Human Rights and Law in China*. Vancouver, Canada: University of British Columbia Press.

Bie, Bijie, and Lu Tang. 2016. "Chinese Gay Men's Coming Out Narratives: Connecting Social Relationship to Co-cultural Theory." *Journal of International and Intercultural Communication* 9 (4): 351–67.

Blee, Kathleen M., and Verta Taylor. 2002. "Semi-Structured Interviewing in Social Movement Research." In *Methods of Social Movement Research*, edited by Bert Klandermans and Suzanne Staggenborg, 92–117. Minneapolis: University of Minnesota Press.

Blumer, Herbert. 1946. "Part Four: Collective Behavior." In *New Outlines of the Principles of Sociology*, edited by A. M. Lee, 167–222. New York: Barnes & Noble.

Boellstorff, Tom. 2005. *The Gay Archipelago: Sexuality and Nation in Indonesia*. Princeton, NJ: Princeton University Press.

Brainer, Amy. 2018. "New Identities or New Intimacies? Rethinking 'Coming Out' in Taiwan through Cross-Generational Ethnography." *Sexualities* 21 (5–6): 914–31.

———. 2019. *Queer Kinship and Family Change in Taiwan*. New Brunswick, NJ: Rutgers.

Campbell-Kibler, Kathryn, Robert Podesva, Sarah Roberts, and Andrew Wong, eds. 2002. *Language and Sexuality: Contesting Meaning in Theory and Practice*. Stanford: CSLI Publications.

Cao, Jin, and Xinlei Lu. 2014. "A Preliminary Exploration of the Gay Movement in Mainland China: Legacy, Transition, Opportunity, and the New Media." *Signs* 39 (4): 840–48.

Carnesecca, Cole. 2015. "Voice of the Masses: The Internet and Responsive Authoritarianism in China." In *Urban Mobilization and New Media in Contemporary China*, edited by Lisheng Dong, Hanspeter Kriesi, and Daniel Kübler, 117–31. Burlington, VT: Ashgate.

Carrillo, Héctor. 1999. "Cultural Change, Hybridity and Male Homosexuality in Mexico." *Culture, Health & Sexuality* 1 (3): 223–38.

Chao, Antonia. 2000. "Global Metaphors and Local Strategies in the Construction of Taiwan's Lesbian Identities." *Culture, Health & Sexuality* 2 (4): 377–90.

Chen, Titus C., and Chia-hao Hsu. 2018. "Double-Speaking Human Rights: Analyzing Human Rights Conception in Chinese Politics (1989–2015)." *Journal of Contemporary China* 27 (112): 534–53.

Chia, Joy L. 2019. "LGBTQ Rights in China: Movement-Building in Uncertain Times." In *Handbook on Human Rights in China*, by Sarah Biddulph and Joshua Rosenzweig, 657–80. Cheltenham, UK: Edward Elgar Publishing.

Chiang, Howard. 2010. "Epistemic Modernity and the Emergence of Homosexuality in China." *Gender & History* 22 (3): 629–57.

Chiang, Howard, and Ari Larissa Heinrich, eds. 2014. *Queer Sinophone Cultures*. New York: Routledge.

Choi, Susanne Y. P., and Ming Luo. 2016. "Performative Family: Homosexuality, Marriage and Intergenerational Dynamics in China." *British Journal of Sociology* 67 (2): 260–80.

Chong, Kee Tan. 2001. "Transcending Sexual Nationalism and Colonialism: Cultural Hybridization as Process of Sexual Politics in '90s Taiwan." In *Postcolonial, Queer: Theoretical Intersections*, edited by John C. Hawley, 123–37. Albany: State University of New York Press.

Chou, Wah-Shan. 2000. *Tongzhi: Politics of Same-Sex Eroticism in Chinese Societies*. New York: Routledge.

———. 2001. "Homosexuality and the Cultural Politics of *Tongzhi* in Chinese Societies." *Journal of Homosexuality* 40 (3–4): 27–46.

Clemens, Elisabeth S. 1993. "Organizational Repertoires and Institutional Change: Women's Groups and the Transformation of American Politics, 1890–1920." *American Journal of Sociology* 98 (4): 755–98.

Cui, Zi'en. 2009. *Zhi Tongzhi* [Queer China, 'Comrade' China]. Beijing: Cuizi DV Studios.

Dai, Jingyun, and Anthony J. Spires. 2018. "Advocacy in an Authoritarian State: How Grassroots Environmental NGOs Influence Local Governments in China." *China Journal* 79 (1): 62–83.

Davis, Joseph E. 2002. "Narrative and Social Movements: The Power of Stories." In *Stories of Change: Narrative and Social Movements*, edited by Joseph E. Davis, 3–29. Albany: State University of New York Press.

Deklerck, Stijn, and Xiaogang Wei. 2015. "Queer Online Media and the Building of China's LGBT Community." In *Queer/Tongzhi China: New Perspectives on Research, Activism and Media Cultures*, edited by Elisabeth L. Engebretsen, William F. Schroeder, and Hongwei Bao, 18–34. Copenhagen: Nordic Institute of Asian Studies.

della Porta, Donatella. 2014. "In-Depth Interviews." In *Methodological Practices in Social Movement Research*, edited by Donatella della Porta, 228–61. Oxford: Oxford University Press.

DeLuca, Kevin Michael, Elizabeth Brunner, and Ye Sun. 2016. "Weibo, WeChat, and the Transformative Events of Environmental Activism on Chinese Wild Public Screens." *International Journal of Communication* 10 (1): 321–39.

De Seta, Gabriele. 2018. "Wenming Bu Wenming: The Socialization of Incivility in Postdigital China." *International Journal of Communication* 12: 2010–30.

Diani, Mario. 1996. "Linking Mobilization Frames and Political Opportunities: Insights from Regional Populism in Italy." *American Sociological Review* 61 (6): 1053–69.

Duggan, Lisa. 2002. *The New Homonormativity: The Sexual Politics of Neoliberalism*. Durham: Duke University Press.

Earl, Jennifer. 2004. "The Cultural Consequences of Social Movements." In *The Blackwell Companion to Social Movements*, edited by David A. Snow, Sarah A. Soule, and Hanspeter Kriesi, 508–30. Oxford: Blackwell.

Engebretsen, Elisabeth L. 2009. "Intimate Practices, Conjugal Ideals: Affective Ties and Relationship Strategies among Lala (Lesbian) Women in Contemporary Beijing." *Sexuality Research and Social Policy* 6 (3): 3–14.

———. 2014. *Queer Women in Urban China: An Ethnography*. New York: Routledge.

Engebretsen, Elisabeth L., William F. Schroeder, and Hongwei Bao, eds. 2015. *Queer/Tongzhi China: New Perspectives on Research, Activism and Media Cultures*. Copenhagen: Nordic Institute of Asian Studies.

Fine, Gary Alan. 1995. "Public Narration and Group Culture: Discerning Discourse in Social Movements." In *Social Movements and Culture*, edited by Hank Johnston and Bert Klandermans, 127–43. Minneapolis: University of Minnesota Press.

Fong, Vanessa L. 2004. *Only Hope: Coming of Age under China's One-Child Policy*. Stanford: Stanford University Press.

Franceschini, Ivan, and Elisa Nesossi. 2018. "State Repression of Chinese Labor NGOs: A Chilling Effect?" *China Journal* 80 (2): 111–29.

Fu, Diana, and Greg Distelhorst. 2017. "Grassroots Participation and Repression under Hu Jintao and Xi Jinping." *China Journal* 79 (1): 100–122.

Fu, Hualing. 2012. "Embedded Socio-Legal Activism in China: The Case of Yirenping." *Hong Kong Law Journal, University of Hong Kong Faculty of Law Research Paper No. 2012/029*: 1–24.

———. 2018. "The July 9th (709) Crackdown on Human Rights Lawyers: Legal Advocacy in an Authoritarian State." *Journal of Contemporary China* 27 (112): 554–68.

Gamson, William A. 1988. "Political Discourse and Collective Action." *International Social Movement Research* 1 (1): 219–44.

Geyer, Robert. 2002. "In Love and Gay." In *Unofficial China in a Globalizing Society*, edited by Perry Link, Richard P. Madsen, and Paul G. Pickowicz, 251–74. Lanham: Rowman and Littlefield.

Grewal, Inderpal, and Caren Kaplan. 2001. "Global Identities: Theorizing Transnational Studies of Sexuality." *GLQ* 7 (4): 663–70.

Guo, Baogang, and Sujian Guo. 2008. *China in Search of a Harmonious Society*. Plymouth, MA: Lexington Books.

Han, Bingfeng, Qianli Yuan, Yuhui Shi, Lai Wei, Jinlin Hou, Jia Shang, Ying Han, et al. 2018. "The Experience of Discrimination of Individuals Living with Chronic Hepatitis B in Four Provinces of China." *PLOS ONE* 13 (4). DOI: 10.1371/journal.pone.0195455.

Harwit, Eric. 2017. "WeChat: Social and Political Development of China's Dominant Messaging App." *Chinese Journal of Communication* 10 (3): 312–27.

Hawley, John C., ed. 2001. *Postcolonial, Queer: Theoretical Intersections.* SUNY Series, Explorations in Postcolonial Studies. Albany: State University of New York Press.

He, Xiaopei, and Susie Jolly. 2002. "Chinese Women Tongzhi Organizing in the 1990s." *Inter-Asia Cultural Studies* 3 (3): 479–91.

Heilmann, Sebastian, and Elizabeth J. Perry, eds. 2011. *Mao's Invisible Hand: The Political Foundations of Adaptive Governance in China.* Cambridge: Harvard University Asia Center.

Hildebrandt, Timothy. 2011. "The Political Economy of Social Organization Registration in China." *China Quarterly* 208 (December): 970–89.

———. 2012. "Development and Division: The Effect of Transnational Linkages and Local Politics on LGBT Activism in China." *Journal of Contemporary China* 21 (77): 845–62.

———. 2013. *Social Organizations and the Authoritarian State in China.* Cambridge: Cambridge University Press.

———. 2018. "NGOs and the Success Paradox: Gay Activism 'after' HIV/AIDS in China." Social Policy Working Paper Series. London School of Economics and Political Science, Department of Social Policy, London.

Hinsch, Bret. 2002. *Passions of the Cut Sleeve: The Male Homosexual Tradition in China.* Berkeley: University of California Press.

Ho, Loretta Wing Wah. 2009. *Gay and Lesbian Subculture in Urban China.* New York: Routledge.

Ho, Peter. 2007. "Embedded Activism and Political Change in a Semiauthoritarian Context." *China Information* 21 (2): 187–209.

Ho, Peter, and Richard Edmonds, eds. 2008. *China's Embedded Activism: Opportunities and Constraints of a Social Movement.* New York: Routledge.

Ho, Petula Sik Ying, Stevi Jackson, Siyang Cao, and Chi Kwok. 2018. "Sex with Chinese Characteristics: Sexuality Research in/on 21st-Century China." *Journal of Sex Research* 55 (4–5): 486–521.

Honig, Emily. 2003. "Socialist Sex: The Cultural Revolution Revisited." *Modern China* 29 (2): 143–75.

Hsing, You-tian, and Ching Kwang Lee, eds. 2009. *Reclaiming Chinese Society: The New Social Activism.* New York: Routledge.

Huang, Shuzhen. 2016. "Post-Oppositional Queer Politics and the Non-confrontational Negotiation of Queer Desires in Contemporary China." Unpublished dissertation, Arizona State University, Phoenix.

Huang, Shuzhen, and Daniel C. Brouwer. 2018. "Coming Out, Coming Home, Coming With: Models of Queer Sexuality in Contemporary China." *Journal of International and Intercultural Communication* 11 (2): 97–116.

Huang, Yixiong. 2018. "Media Representation of Tongxinglian in China: A Case Study of the People's Daily." *Journal of Homosexuality* 65 (3): 338–60.

Jacka, Tamara. 2009. "Cultivating Citizens: *Suzhi* (Quality) Discourse in the PRC." *Positions: East Asia Cultures Critique* 17 (3): 523–35.

Jackson, Peter A. 2001. "Pre-Gay, Post-Queer: Thai Perspectives on Proliferating Gender/Sex Diversity in Asia." *Journal of Homosexuality* 40 (3–4): 1–25.

Jasper, James M. 1997. *The Art of Moral Protest: Culture, Biography, and Creativity in Social Movements*. Chicago: University of Chicago Press.

———. 1998. "The Emotions of Protest: Affective and Reactive Emotions in and around Social Movements." *Sociological Forum* 13 (3): 397–421.

Jenkins, Craig J. 1983. "Resource Mobilization Theory and the Study of Social Movements." *Annual Review of Sociology* 9 (1): 527–53.

Johnson, Mark, Peter Jackson, and Gilbert Herdt. 2000. "Critical Regionalities and the Study of Gender and Sexual Diversity in South East and East Asia." *Culture, Health & Sexuality* 2 (4): 361–75.

Johnston, Hank, ed. 2009. *Culture, Social Movements, and Protest*. Burlington, VT: Ashgate.

Kahlina, Katja. 2015. "Local Histories, European LGBT Designs: Sexual Citizenship, Nationalism, and 'Europeanisation' in Post-Yugoslav Croatia and Serbia." *Women's Studies International Forum* 49: 73–83.

Kam, Lucetta Yip Lo. 2013. *Shanghai Lalas: Female* Tongzhi *Communities and Politics in Urban China*. Hong Kong: Hong Kong University Press.

Kane, Anne E. 1997. "Theorizing Meaning Construction in Social Movements: Symbolic Structures and Interpretation during the Irish Land War, 1879–1882." *Sociological Theory* 15 (3): 249–76.

Kang, Wenqing. 2009. *Obsession: Male Same-Sex Relations in China, 1900–1950*. Hong Kong: Chinese University of Hong Kong Press.

Keck, Margaret E., and Kathryn Sikkink. 1998. *Activists beyond Borders: Advocacy Networks in International Politics*. Ithaca, NY: Cornell University Press.

Keech-Marx, Samantha. 2008. "Airing Dirty Laundry in Public: Anti-Domestic Violence Activism in Beijing." In *Associations and the Chinese State: Contested Spaces*, edited by Jonathan Unger, 187–211. New York: Routledge.

Kim-Puri, H. J. 2005. "Conceptualizing Gender-Sexuality-State-Nation: An Introduction." *Gender & Society* 19 (2): 137–59.

Kong, Travis S. K. 2010. *Chinese Male Homosexualities: Memba, Tongzhi and Golden Boy*. Routledge Contemporary China Series. New York: Routledge.

———. 2016. "The Sexual in Chinese Sociology: Homosexuality Studies in Contemporary China." *Sociological Review* 64 (3): 495–514.

———. 2020. "Towards a Transnational Queer Sociology: Historical Formation of *Tongzhi* Identities and Cultures in Hong Kong and Taiwan (1980s–1990s) and China (late 1990s–early 2000s)." *Journal of Homosexuality*: 1–25.

Kong, Travis S. K., Sky H. L. Lau, and Amory H. W. Hui. 2019. "Tongzhi." In *Global Encyclopedia of Lesbian, Gay, Bisexual, Transgender, and Queer History*, edited by Howard Chiang, Anjali Arondekar, Marc Epprecht, Jennifer Evans, Ross G. Forman, Hanadi Al-Samman, Emily Skidmore, and Zeb Tortorici. New York: Scribner.

Kubal, Timothy J. 1998. "The Presentation of Political Self: Cultural Resonance and the Construction of Collective Action Frames." *Sociological Quarterly* 39:539–54.

Kwong, Julia. 1988. "The 1986 Student Demonstrations in China: A Democratic Movement?" *Asian Survey* 28 (9): 970–85.

Leap, William L., and Tom Boellstorff, eds. 2004. *Speaking in Queer Tongues: Globalization and Gay Language*. Chicago: University of Illinois Press.

Le Bon, Gustave. 1896. *The Crowd: Study of the Popular Mind*. Mineola, DE: Dover Publications.

Lei, Ya-Wen. 2018. *The Contentious Public Sphere: Law, Media, and Authoritarian Rule in China*. Princeton, NJ: Princeton University Press.

Leung, Helen Hok-Sze. 2008. *Undercurrents: Queer Culture and Postcolonial Hong Kong*. Vancouver, Canada: University of British Columbia Press.

Liao, Sara. 2019. "'#IAmGay# What About You?': Storytelling, Discursive Politics, and the Affective Dimension of Social Media Activism against Censorship in China." *International Journal of Communication* 13 (21): 2314–33.

Lim, Song Hwee. 2008. "How to Be Queer in Taiwan: Translation, Appropriation, and the Construction of a Queer Identity in Taiwan." In *AsiaPacifiQueer: Rethinking Genders and Sexualities*, edited by Fran Martin et al., 235–50. Chicago: University of Illinois Press.

Liu, Jen-peng, and Nafei Ding. 2005. "Reticent Poetics, Queer Politics." *Inter-Asia Cultural Studies* 6 (1): 30–55.

Liu, Jun. 2019a. "Digital Media, Cycles of Contention, and Urban Governance in China: Anti-PX Protests as an Example of the Sustainability of Environmental Activism." In *Greening China's Urban Governance: Tackling Environmental and Sustainability Challenges*, edited by Jørgen Delman, Yuan Ren, Outi Luova, Mattias Burell, and Oscar Almén, 177–93. Springer Asia Series. Singapore: Springer Singapore.

———. 2019b. "From Mobilization to Legitimation: Digital Media and the Evolving Repertoire of Contention in Contemporary China." In *Handbook of Protest and Resistance in China*, edited by Teresa Wright, 332–45. Cheltenham, UK: Edward Elgar Publishing.

Liu, Peter, and Lisa Rofel. 2010. "Beyond the Strai(Gh)Ts: Transnationalism and Queer Chinese Politics." *Positions: East Asia Cultures Critique* 18 (2): 281–89.

Long, Yan. 2018. "The Contradictory Impact of Transnational AIDS Institutions on State Repression in China, 1989–2013." *American Journal of Sociology* 124 (2): 309–66.

Ma, Qiusha. 2005. *Non-Governmental Organizations in Contemporary China: Paving the Way to Civil Society?* New York: Routledge.

Manderson, Lenore, and Margaret Jolly. 1997. *Sites of Desire/Economies of Pleasure: Sexualities in Asia and the Pacific.* Chicago: University of Chicago Press.

Mannoni, Michele. 2019. "*Hefa Quanyi*: More Than a Problem of Translation; Linguistic Evidence of Lawfully Limited Rights in China." *International Journal for the Semiotics of Law* 32 (1): 29–46.

Marquis, Christopher, and Yanhua Bird. 2018. "The Paradox of Responsive Authoritarianism: How Civic Activism Spurs Environmental Penalties in China." *Organization Science* 29 (5): 948–68.

McAdam, Doug. 1982. *Political Process and the Development of Black Insurgency.* Chicago: University of Chicago Press.

McAdam, Doug, John McCarthy, and Mayer Zald, eds. 1996. *Comparative Perspectives on Social Movements: Political Opportunities, Mobilizing Structures, and Cultural Framings.* New York: Cambridge University Press.

Meyer, David S., and Nancy Whittier. 1994. "Social Movement Spillover." *Social Problems* 41 (2): 277–98.

Munson, Ziad. 2009. *The Making of Pro-Life Activists: How Social Movement Mobilization Works.* Chicago: University of Chicago Press.

O'Brien, Kevin J., and Lianjiang Li. 2006. *Rightful Resistance in Rural China.* Cambridge: Cambridge University Press.

O'Brien, Kevin J., and Rachel Stern. 2008. "Studying Contention in Contemporary China." In *Popular Protest in China*, edited by Kevin J. O'Brien, 11–25. Cambridge, MA: Harvard University Press.

Oliver, Pamela E., and Hank Johnston. 2000. "What a Good Idea! Ideologies and Frames in Social Movement Research." *Mobilization* 5 (1): 37–54.

Oswin, Natalie. 2004. "Decentering Queer Globalization: Diffusion and the 'Global Gay.'" *Environment and Planning D: Society and Space* 24 (5): 777–90.

Pan, Suiming, and Yingying Huang. 2013.《性之变：21世纪中国人的性生活》 [*Changes in Sex: The Sexual Life of the Chinese in the Twenty-First Century*]. Beijing: Renmin University of China Press.

Park, Robert E. 1927. "Human Nature and Collective Behavior." *American Journal of Sociology* 32 (5): 733–41.

Parkin, Siodhbhra. 2018. "LGBT Rights-Focused Legal Advocacy in China: The Promise, and Limits, of Litigation." *Fordham International Law Journal* 41 (5): 1243–62.

Perry, Elizabeth J. 2001. *Challenging the Mandate of Heaven: Social Protest and State Power in China.* New York: M. E. Sharpe.

———. 2007. "Studying Chinese Politics: Farewell to Revolution?" *China Journal* 57 (1): 1–22.

Piccone, Ted. 2018. "China's Long Game on Human Rights at the United Nations." *Foreign Policy at Brookings, Foreign Policy Paper Series On International*

Governance: 1–21. https://www.brookings.edu/wp-content/uploads/2018
/09/FP_20181009_china_human_rights.pdf.

Pils, Eva. 2019. "Human Rights and the Political System." In *Handbook on Human Rights in China*, by Sarah Biddulph and Joshua Rosenzweig, 32–59. Cheltenham, UK: Edward Elgar Publishing.

Plows, Alexandra. 2008. "Social Movements and Ethnographic Methodologies: An Analysis Using Case Study Examples." *Sociology Compass* 2 (5): 1523–38.

Polletta, Francesca. 2002. "Plotting Protest: Mobilizing Stories in the 1960 Student Sit-Ins." In *Stories of Change: Narrative and Social Movements*, edited by Joseph E. Davis, 31–51. Albany: State University of New York Press.

———. 2006. *It Was Like a Fever: Storytelling in Protest and Politics*. Chicago: University of Chicago Press.

———. 2008. "Culture and Movements." *The ANNALS of the American Academy of Political and Social Science* 619 (1): 78–96.

———. 2012. "Three Mechanisms by Which Culture Shapes Movement Strategy: Repertoires, Institutional Norms, and Metonymy." In *Strategies for Social Change: Social Movement, Protest, and Contention*, vol. 37, edited by Gregory M. Maney, Rachel V. Kutz-Flamenbaum, Deana A. Rohlinger, and Jeff Goodwin, 43–57. Minneapolis, University of Minnesota Press.

Polletta, Francesca, and James M. Jasper. 2001. "Collective Identity and Social Movements." *Annual Review of Sociology* 27 (1): 283–305.

Powell, Brian, Natasha Yurk Quadlin, and Oren Pizmony-Levy. 2015. "Public Opinion, the Courts, and Same-Sex Marriage: Four Lessons Learned." *Social Currents* 2 (1): 3–12.

Puar, Jasbir. 2007. *Terrorist Assemblages: Homonationalism in Queer Times*. Durham: Duke University Press.

———. 2011. "Citation and Censorship: The Politics of Talking about the Sexual Politics of Israel." *Feminist Legal Studies* 19 (2): 133–42.

Puar, Jasbir, and Maya Mikdashi. 2012. "Pinkwatching and Pinkwashing: Interpenetration and Its Discontents." *Jadaliyya*. https://www.jadaliyya.com/Details/26818.

Pugh, Allison J. 2013. "What Good Are Interviews for Thinking about Culture? Demystifying Interpretive Analysis." *American Journal of Cultural Sociology* 1 (1): 42–68.

Qiaoan, Runya, and Jessica C. Teets. 2020. "Responsive Authoritarianism in China—A Review of Responsiveness in Xi and Hu Administrations." *Journal of Chinese Political Science* 25 (1): 139–53.

Rauchfleisch, Adrian, and Mike S. Schäfer. 2015. "Multiple Public Spheres of Weibo: A Typology of Forms and Potentials of Online Public Spheres in China." *Information, Communication & Society* 18 (2): 139–55.

Richardson, Diane. 2017. "Rethinking Sexual Citizenship." *Sociology* 51 (2): 208–24.

Rofel, Lisa. 1999. "Qualities of Desire: Imagining Gay Identities in China." *GLQ* 5 (4): 451–74.

———. 2007. *Desiring China: Experiments in Neoliberalism, Sexuality, and Public Culture.* Duke University Press.

Rojas, Fabio. 2007. *From Black Power to Black Studies: How a Radical Social Movement Became an Academic Discipline.* Baltimore: Johns Hopkins University Press.

Sang, Tze-Lan D. 2003. *The Emerging Lesbian: Same-Sex Desire in Modern China.* Chicago: University of Chicago Press.

Savci, Evren. 2021. *Queer in Translation: Sexual Politics under Neoliberal Islam.* Durham, NC: Duke University Press.

Schotten, C. Heike. 2016. "Homonationalism: From Critique to Diagnosis, or, We Are All Homonationals Now." *International Feminist Journal of Politics* 18 (3): 351–70.

Sinnott, Megan. 2012. "Korean-Pop, *Tom Gay Kings, Les Queens* and the Capitalist Transformation of Sex/Gender Categories in Thailand." *Asian Studies Review* 36 (4): 453–74.

Snow, David A., and Robert D. Benford. 1988. "Ideology, Frame Resonance, and Participant Mobilization." *Interdisciplinary Social Movement Research* 1 (1): 197–218.

———. 1992. "Master Frames and Cycles of Protest." In *Frontiers in Social Movement Theory*, edited by Aldon D. Morris and Carol McClurg Mueller, 133–55. New Haven, CT: Yale University Press.

Spires, Anthony J. 2011. "Contingent Symbiosis and Civil Society in an Authoritarian State: Understanding the Survival of China's Grassroots NGOs." *American Journal of Sociology* 117 (1): 1–45.

Stein, Michael Ashley. 2010. "China and Disability Rights." *Loyola of Los Angeles International and Comparative Law Review* 33 (7): 7–26.

Steinberg, Marc W. 1998. "Tilting the Frame: Considerations on Collective Action Framing from a Discursive Turn." *Theory and Society* 27 (6): 845–72.

Tai, Zixue. 2006. *The Internet in China: Cyberspace and Civil Society.* New York: Routledge.

Tamura, Eileen H., Linda K. Menton, Noren W. Lush, Francis K. C. Tsui, and Warren Cohen. 1997. *China: Understanding Its Past.* Honolulu: University of Hawai'i Press.

Tanner, Harold M. 2000. "The Offense of Hooliganism and the Moral Dimension of China's Pursuit of Modernity, 1979–1996." *Twentieth-Century China* 26 (1): 1–40.

Tanner, Murray Scot. 2000. "State Coercion and the Balance of Awe: The 1983–1986 'Stern Blows' Anti-Crime Campaign." *China Journal* 44 (2): 93–125.

Tarrow, Sidney. 1994. *Power in Movement: Social Movements and Contentious Politics.* New York: Cambridge University Press.

———. 2013. *The Language of Contention: Revolutions in Words, 1688–2012*. New York: Cambridge University Press.

Taylor, Verta, and Nella Van Dyke. 2004. "Get Up, Stand Up: Technical Repertoires of Social Movements." In *The Blackwell Companion to Social Movements*, edited by David A. Snow, Sarah A. Soule, and Hanspeter Kriesi, 262–93. Oxford: Blackwell.

Taylor, Verta, and Nancy Whittier. 1995. "Analytical Approaches to Social Movement Culture: The Culture of the Women's Movement." In *Social Movements and Culture*, edited by Hank Johnston and Bert Klandermans, 163–87. Minneapolis: University of Minnesota Press.

Teets, Jessica C. 2013. "Let Many Civil Societies Bloom: The Rise of Consultative Authoritarianism in China." *China Quarterly* 213 (March): 19–38.

———. 2014. *Civil Society under Authoritarianism: The China Model.* Cambridge: Cambridge University Press.

Thoreson, Ryan R. 2014. *Transnational LGBT Activism: Working for Sexual Rights Worldwide.* Minneapolis: University of Minnesota Press.

Thornton, Margaret R. ed. 2002. *Romancing the Tomes: Popular Culture, Law and Feminism.* London: Cavendish Publishing.

Tian, Ian Liujia. 2019. "Graduated In/Visibility: Reflections on *Ku'er* Activism in (Post)Socialist China." *QED* 6 (3): 56–75.

Tilly, Charles. 2008. *Contentious Performances.* New York: Cambridge University Press.

Tilly, Charles, and Sidney Tarrow. 2006. *Contentious Politics.* Boulder: Paradigm Publishers.

Tomba, Luigi. 2009. "Of Quality, Harmony, and Community: Civilization and the Middle Class in Urban China." *Positions: East Asia Cultures Critique* 17 (3): 591–616.

Tsui, Lokman. 2003. "The Panopticon as the Antithesis of a Space of Freedom: Control and Regulation of the Internet in China." *China Information* 17 (2): 65–82.

Tu, Fangjing. 2016. "WeChat and Civil Society in China." *Communication and the Public* 1 (3): 343–50.

United Nations Development Programme (UNDP). 2016. *Being LGBTI in China—A National Survey on Social Attitudes towards Sexual Orientation, Gender Identity and Gender Expression.* https://www.undp.org/china/publications/being-lgbti-china.

Van Dyke, Nella, and Verta Taylor. 2018. "The Cultural Outcomes of Social Movements." In *The Wiley Blackwell Companion to Social Movements*, edited by David A. Snow, Sarah A. Soule, Hanspeter Kriesi, and Holly J. McCammon, 482–98. Chichester, UK: John Wiley & Sons.

Wang, Jing. 2019. *The Other Digital China: Nonconfrontational Activism on the Social Web.* Cambridge, MA: Harvard University Press.

Wang, Shaoguang, and Jianyu He. 2004. "Associational Revolution in China: Mapping the Landscapes." *Korea Observer* 35 (3): 485–533.

Wang, Zheng. 2014. "The Chinese Dream: Concept and Context." *Journal of Chinese Political Science* 19 (1): 1–13.

Wei, Wei. 2007. "'Wandering Men' No Longer Wander Around: The Production and Transformation of Local Homosexual Identities in Contemporary Chengdu, China." *Inter-Asia Cultural Studies* 8 (4): 572–88.

Williams, Rhys H. 1995. "Constructing the Public Good: Cultural Resources and Social Movements." *Social Problems* 42 (1): 124–44.

———. 2004. "The Cultural Contexts of Collective Action: Constraints, Opportunities, and the Symbolic Life of Social Movements." In *The Blackwell Companion to Social Movements*, edited by David A. Snow, Sarah A. Soule, and Hanspeter Kriesi, 91–115. Oxford: Blackwell.

Wong, Andrew D. 2004. "Language, Cultural Authenticity, and the *Tongzhi* Movement." *Texas Linguistic Forum* 48, Proceedings of the Twelfth Annual Symposium about Language and Society, Austin, April 16–18, 209–15.

———. 2005. "The Reappropriation of *Tongzhi*." *Language in Society* 34 (5): 763–93.

Wong, Day. 2007. "Rethinking the Coming Home Alternative: Hybridization and Coming out Politics in Hong Kong's Anti-homophobia Parades." *Inter-Asia Cultural Studies* 8 (4): 600–616.

———. 2016. "Sexology and the making of sexual subjects in contemporary China." *Journal of Sociology* 52 (1): 68–82.

Woodman, Sophia. 2015. "Segmented Publics and the Regulation of Critical Speech in China." *Asian Studies Review* 39 (1): 100–118.

Worth, Heather, Jing Jing, Karen McMillan, Chunyan Su, Xiaoxing Fu, Zhang Yuping, Rui Zhao, Jia Cui, Angela Kelly-Hanku and Zhang Youchun. 2017. "Under the Same Quilt: The Paradoxes of Sex between Men in the Cultural Revolution." *Journal of Homosexuality* 64 (1): 61–74.

Wu, Fengshi. 2017. "An Emerging Group Name 'Gongyi': Ideational Collectivity in China's Civil Society." *China Review* 17 (2): 123–50.

Yang, Guobin. 2005. "Environmental NGOs and Institutional Dynamics in China." *China Quarterly* 181 (March): 46–66.

———. 2009. *The Power of the Internet in China: Citizen Activism Online*. New York: Columbia University Press.

Yu, Xuanmeng, and Xirong He, eds. 2007. *Shanghai: Its Urbanization and Culture*. Washington: Council for Research in Values and Philosophy.

Yue, Audrey, and Helen Hok-Sze Leung. 2017. "Notes towards the Queer Asian City: Singapore and Hong Kong." *Urban Studies* 54 (3): 747–64.

Yuen, Samson. 2015. "Friend or Foe? The Diminishing Space of China's Civil Society." *China Perspectives* 3: 51–56.

Zeng, Fanxu, and Yu Huang. 2015. "The Media and Urban Contention in China: A Co-empowerment Model." *Chinese Journal of Communication* 8 (3): 233–52.

Zhang, Chao. 2017. "'Nothing about Us without Us': The Emerging Disability Movement and Advocacy in China." *Disability & Society* 32 (7): 1096–101.

Zhang, Jingsheng. 1926. *Xing Shi [Sex Histories]*. China: Taibei Shi.

Zhao, Dingxin. 2001. *The Power of Tiananmen: State-Society Relations and the 1989 Beijing Student Movement*. Chicago: University of Chicago Press.

Zhao, Suisheng. 2016. "The Ideological Campaign in Xi's China: Rebuilding Regime Legitimacy." *Asian Survey* 56 (6): 1168–93.

Zhao, Xintong, and Chao Zhang. 2018. "From Isolated Fence to Inclusive Society: The Transformational Disability Policy in China." *Disability & Society* 33 (1): 132–37.

Zhao, Yuezhi. 2008. *Communication in China: Political Economy, Power, and Conflict*. Lanham: Rowman & Littlefield.

Zheng, Tiantian. 2009. *Red Lights: The Lives of Sex Workers in Postsocialist China*. Minneapolis: University of Minnesota Press.

———. 2015. *Tongzhi Living: Men Attracted to Men in Postsocialist China*. Minneapolis: University of Minnesota Press.

Zheng, Yongnian. 2007. *Technological Empowerment: The Internet, State, and Society in China*. Stanford: Stanford University Press.

Zhou, Mujun. 2018. "Fissures between Human Rights Advocates and NGO Practitioners in China's Civil Society: A Case Study of the Equal Education Campaign, 2009–2013." *China Quarterly* 234 (June): 486–505.

Index

Caterina Fugazzola is Assistant Senior Instructional Professor of Global Studies at the University of Chicago.

www.ingramcontent.com/pod-product-compliance
Lightning Source LLC
Chambersburg PA
CBHW020704270326
41928CB00005B/265